The Rusticator's Journal

A collection of articles from
the *Journal* of Friends of Acadia

Edited by Tammis E. Coffin

Friends of Acadia, August 1993
Text copyright ©1993 by Friends of Acadia

Published by Friends of Acadia
Bar Harbor, Maine

Design by Z Studio

ISBN 0-9637694-0-5

DEDICATION

To Charles R. Tyson, Jr. – his family goes back to the beginning, with a legacy that continues into the future. He is descended from John Roebling and Robert Fulton, and his grandfather, Carroll S. Tyson, Jr. was one of Mount Desert Island's pre-eminent artists of the nineteenth century. Charlie's dedication, enthusiasm, and talent are leading us in preserving this magnificent island for the future.

The Cobblestone Bridge is one of 17 bridges found along Acadia National Park's carriage roads. This beautiful network of unpaved roads was donated to Acadia National Park by John D. Rockefeller, Jr. for use by walkers, hikers and non-motorized vehicles. The carriage roads are currently being restored by the National Park Service and Friends of Acadia.

Table of Contents

contents continued

contents continued

contents continued

Introduction

MT. DESERT ISLAND has always been a destination for the robust and hearty individual. Its rocky coast, its rugged mountains, and its daunting trails do not lure that person who prefers to lie about on a sandy beach, wade in tepid water, or walk through placid glade. No, Mt. Desert Island is for the strong of spirit, those who desire to be challenged by the terrain and the elements.

The island has a long history. Like many places, it has harbored generations of contented inhabitants who, because their lives engendered no notoriety, simply became footnotes on the pages of history. Mt. Desert Island has been discovered many times by new and different types of people. The discovery of Mt. Desert Island that led it to its destiny, at least that which we presently know, was accomplished by a group known as the "rusticators".

Among those usually named as the first of the rusticators is the artist Thomas Cole. A member of the Hudson River School of landscape painting, he came to Mount Desert Island in 1844 and proceeded to glorify the island on canvas. His work inspired a host of other artists to follow, most notable being Frederic Church. Soon writers, naturalists, students, adventurers, and sportsmen came to enjoy this paradise for themselves.

This hearty breed thrived on the rustic life. They enthusiastically accepted the crude accommodations and simple food provided by local fisherman and farmers. These natives, happy to have some extra cash, gladly provided hospitality as they knew it. Their relationship comes down to us as having been wonderfully symbiotic. Simple folk shared a pastoral life-style in the midst of bounteous nature with an adventurist intellectual elite.

Like all good things, Mount Desert Island with its life-style was discovered by more and more people until it became something quite different than what it had been. Hotels were built, transportation was improved, and the tourist industry on Mt. Desert Island was born.

Since that time entire eras have come and gone. Beginning in the 1870's, there were the big hotel years, followed by the Gilded Age with its magnificent cottages, and over the past eight decades there has been the development of Acadia National Park as the focal point of the island. Recently we have seen the burgeoning of the modern tourist era with millions of visitors descending yearly upon this island with its rugged features and fragile ecology. Despite this, most of the island's charms survive and there exists an active movement to make certain they remain in perpetuity.

Friends of Acadia is an organization dedicated to preserving and protecting the heritage and traditions of this magnificent island and its national park. The reader will find in this volume a collection of writings from our JOURNAL. We have assembled this collection so that today's visitor can come to understand the past, and even more importantly, appreciate that this

Summer life at its brightest, under the shadow of Mount Desert's green hills. Canoeists in Frenchman Bay during the hotel era.

area retains its magnificence. And then we sincerely hope that you, the reader, will join us in the spirit of the rusticators and help us to make certain this island, this natural masterpiece, will always possess those unique qualities that attracted all this attention, so that generations and generations from now, people will still proclaim its wonders.

Let us all assume the spirit of the rusticators and resist attempts to tame this place.

– D.P.

Newport Mountain, considered by many rusticators the most picturesque and pleasing elevation on the island, is now called Champlain Mountain. The mountain is a solid mass of granite, bare on top, and commands a noble view of islands and ocean.

Cloud Caps Over The Porcupines

by Emma Farway

ON OTHERWISE CLOUDLESS SUMMER mornings, small dome-shaped clouds form directly above the tree-tops over each of the small Porcupine Islands in Frenchman Bay. These cloud caps, as I call them, vanish early in the afternoon, with the first breath of wind.

In June and July, the clouds caps happen more often and sometimes reoccur for days in succession, drawing the attention and wonder of all who see them. Some years, without the right conditions, we might not see these special clouds all summer long.

Here on Mt. Desert Island we see plenty of fog each summer, and it comes in many forms. There is the high fog that lingers around the mountain tops after it rains, the offshore fog that creeps into the bays at night and recedes early in the day, and the morning fog that lingers as a thin mist over the water, pierced by the masts of sailboats. In winter only, on the coldest days, when the temperature is far below zero, wisps of "sea smoke" rise from the water; not fog but steam, formed because the air is so much colder than the sea.

But our cloud caps are in a category all their own. They are more similar to high altitude clouds in the mountainous regions of the world than they are to fog along the coast of Maine. In form they closely resemble what are called "wave clouds," formed when vapor-saturated air is blown over high mountain peaks. Their appearance in Frenchman Bay is brought about when moisture-laden air moving across the surface of the ocean must rise to pass over the steep-sided Porcupine Islands. In that short distance, if the temperatures are right and winds are still, the moist air expands and cools and condenses in the form of a cloud.

When I first came to Mt. Desert Island, I saw them — miniature clouds, poised like flying saucers over each small island in the bay. I gazed at them spellbound, thinking, "This place is magic." Others I have spoken to agree... it is a beautiful, mystifying thing. You never quite know when the cloud caps are going to appear, but having seen them once, you always hope that you will see them again. ❧

Clouds among the Porcupine Islands, named for the animal whose shape they resemble.

Looking west to Eagle Lake from the Green Mountain road, now called the Cadillac Mountain road.

The Green Mountain Robbery

by Gladys O'Neil

NOT ALL OF THE highway robberies in the 1880's took-place in the wild, wild West. One such robbery took place on August 2nd in 1882 at one o'clock in the afternoon on the Green (now Cadillac) Mountain road.

Isaac and John How, two of Bar Harbor's best known summer residents, accompanied by two ladies, whose names were never disclosed, had been on a buckboard drive to the summit of Green Mountain. When they had driven a short distance down the mountain, a man stepped out of the woods and ordered their driver,

Chauncey Joy, to stop the horses, which he did. The person was said to have been of medium height and well built. He did not wear a hat, but had a piece of cloth over his head which reached to his shoulders. His eyes were visible through two holes that were cut through the front of the material. He wore a printed shirt, loose and belted at the waist. There was a large pistol in the belt and another in his hand.

The masked man walked around to the side of the buckboard and placed his pistol about four inches from

16

John How's head and asked him for his money. Mr. How passed him his pocketbook. The robber then asked for his "keeper," pointing to his watch. Mr. How passed it to him. Walking over to Isaac How, he ordered him to hand over his money. Isaac's pocketbook appeared to be nearly empty, which did not go unnoticed by the thief, as he then asked for the money in his back pocket and was given six hundred dollars in bills. When asked for his keeper, Isaac How parted with it reluctantly, as it

A shelter for overnight guests at summit of Green Mountain, built by Daniel Brewer at the close of the rusticator era in 1861.

was an unusually beautiful gold watch. The ladies were prepared to part with their jewelry and money, but the robber said, "We never trouble ladies," and then disappeared into the woods from which he had come. The group continued their drive down the mountain and reported the robbery immediately upon their arrival back in the village.

The news of the robbery was sent quickly to all the towns in the area, and a large search party went up the mountain to find the thief. Buckboard parties were formed and went in immediate pursuit, but found no one.

The event caused great excitement. The telegraph office was soon besieged by reporters attempting to wire their papers. The correspondent for the *New York Herald* tried in vain to send in his story and mailed it instead. The Sunday *Boston Globe* carried a long account of the robbery. Other papers telegraphed to have all particulars sent on.

There seemed to be a general agreement that the robber was a professional and probably a Westerner because of his use of the word "keeper." Many people expressed the opinion that he was probably sitting on the porch of one of the hotels, relaxing and enjoying the excitement that he had caused. John and Isaac How offered a reward of $5,000 for his detection and conviction, and many summer residents and shop keepers, whose names appeared in the *Mt. Desert Herald*, joined in contributing to the fund. Amateur and professional detectives soon arrived on the scene, and it wasn't long before there were rumors that they had spotted the man. Meanwhile, sales of revolvers in the town increased considerably.

As might be expected, any unusual happening created rumors. There were reports of suspicious looking characters running across fields or appearing from the woods. One such person was said to be hanging around

TO THE
MT. DESERT TOURIST
YOU HAVE **NOT SEEN** MT. DESERT
UNTIL YOU HAVE VIEWED IT FROM THE
SUMMIT
OF
GREEN MOUNTAIN
1525 FEET ABOVE THE SEA LEVEL.
This elevation, affording the most Extensive and Beautiful View upon the Atlantic Coast,
IS REACHED BY AN EASY DRIVE
VIA THE
Green Mountain Carriage Toll Road.
For further particulars ask any Buckboard Driver
A Good Hotel on the Summit.

Buckboard drives up Green Mountain were a popular activity during the hotel era.

17

Green's Landing on Deer Isle. Four men were seen leaving Bar Harbor on a schooner, but only three were on the boat when it arrived in Rockland, and those men refused to account for the fourth man. And then there was the boat that was stolen and taken over to Ironbound Island for a few days and later left somewhere near Seal Cove.

The *Mt. Desert Herald* made this statement in their August 4th edition: "Some of our visiting friends seem surprised at the large amount offered as a reward for the arrest and conviction of the man who committed the highway robbery on Green Mountain, but it should be remembered that both the citizens and summer sojourners at Bar Harbor are very much interested in this matter.

Similar crimes will not be attempted very soon here as the imitator of the late Jesse James would meet a decidedly warm reception, but if the man who did this thing could be caught, an example will be made of him as a warning that thereafter the State Prison for life awaits him if detected, and our people mean to make it an object for detectives, both amateur and professional, to spend their time tracing him."

Indeed the robber might well have been imprisoned for life, as that was the punishment for such a crime committed in the State of Maine; however, the thief covered his tracks well and was never apprehended. It was the last robbery of its kind on Green Mountain. ❧

Green Mountain, now called Cadillac, is the highest point on the east coast of the United States. Those who greet dawn at its summit may be the first in the nation to see the sun rise, depending on the time of year.

THE BAR HARBOR MOUNTAINS, MAINE

Once There Was Robin Hood Park

by Percy Greer

NO MATTER WHERE ONE pauses to stop and look in the town of Bar Harbor, one's eyes fall upon a picture that has been repainted many times. Whatever is there now was not there in the previous era, and what was there then was not there before.

Each time I drive by the Bluenose Ferry Terminal I try to imagine what it was like when Wingwood House stood on that very site. This building had eighty rooms (plus a thirty room servants' quarters), 28 bathrooms with gold fixtures, and 26 hand carved marble fireplaces imported from Europe. It was built by the E.T. Stotesburys in 1925. Unlike so many of Bar Harbor's great cottages it survived the 1947 fire only to be torn down in 1953.

Even harder to imagine is Robin Hood Park. Today one looks upon its site and sees the vast Jackson Laboratory complex. But, for twelve years, from 1900 to 1912, the nation's elite gathered there for three days

Viewed from Newport Mountain is the oval track at Robin Hood Park, once the gathering place of the nation's elite and now the location of the Jackson Laboratory.

19

each August for the annual Horse Show.

The park was owned by Colonel Edward Morrell of Philadelphia. Himself an avid horseman, he was delighted to make the park and its oval track available to the Horse Show and Fair Association. Socialites came from all the east coast summer communities, Southampton, Newport, and the North Shore, to enjoy themselves and compete. The affair was financed by selling viewing boxes, each containing eight folding chairs, for $500 for the three days. This is comparable to $50,000 in 1993!

A couple of reminiscences from those days have been left to us by Chester Wescott:

"Ed McLeon, who had purchased the Montgomery Sears estate on the Shore Path, got the idea into his head that he would put a few of the old-timers like Philip Livingston, Colonel Morrell, Ketterlinus, Pulitzers, and a few others who always walked away with the blue ribbons, to shame. He sent over to England and purchased the finest horseflesh possible. Entered them. He had a big tent just behind the grandstand, and I recall riding down to the Robin Hood Park in a cart with at least twenty-four cases of beer for his attendants. It was really something to see. He engaged Eleonora Sears and Dorothy Forbes from Boston to drive with him. Believe it or not, every time they appeared before the judges' stand, Ed won all the blue ribbons. He would tip that old felt hat he wore in acknowledgement, which was rather amusing to the spectators."

He tells another tale of remarkable social savvy: "Mr. Pineo was in charge of the Horse Show. David Rodick was his nephew and helped him with his duties. I remember one day they were making up the program and Pineo was going to put Edsel Ford's children and the Rockefeller children with their pony carriages in the same class. In competition. Dave immediately shouted, 'You're crazy, don't do that! Put them in separate classes, so that each can get a blue ribbon and cup. We need their box money to finance this show and you will ruin everything.' This was done and everyone was happy."

The spectator can only wonder what the viewer will see one hundred years hence. 🍂

The annual Bar Harbor Horse Show took place in August from 1900 to 1912. Each viewing box containing eight folding chairs cost $500 for the three days.

The Rusticators And The Abenaki

by Kathryn Harmon

THERE SEEM TO BE as many different opinions on the actual dates of the Rusticator's Era as there are people with opinions. Yet, there is no dispute that a gradual shift in the late 1870's and 1880's replaced Bar Harbor's rusticators with hotel guests. This change manifested itself in, among other things, the lives of the members of the Passamaquoddy, Penobscot, and St. James River tribes. These native people, collectively called the Abenaki, had been setting up their summer camps in Bar Harbor as long as anyone could remember.

Early yachtsmen and sportsmen came to Mt. Desert Island by sea and were met on shore by native tribes who appreciated the same things these visitors came to enjoy. Mt. Desert Island and its surrounding waters had opportunities for hunting and fishing, actively sought by sportsmen and practiced by the Indians. What ensued was a trade relationship through which the Abenaki showed the visitor where and how to most successfully hunt and fish. In return, the visitors would give wares from their homelands or share some of the profits of a good hunt.

As visitors to Mt. Desert Island became more numerous and the hotel industry flourished, Indian access to the land became more constricted. The priorities of the people coming to visit were changing, along with their ideas about how to use the land. The earlier groups of visitors associated closely with the Indians, while new, more cosmopolitan visitors were not as interested in guidance from the Abenaki.

In the 1870's there was an Indian encampment located at the foot of Holland Avenue at the intersection with West Street. There, the relationship between Indian and traveler changed from barter to cash. Sweetgrass baskets, birch-bark baskets, moccasins and seal skins were sold. The Indians had become a commercial business. They even advertised in the *Mt. Desert Herald*.

In 1884 arrangements were made to bring electricity to the encampment. The camp was open to visitors on pleasant evenings until half-past ten o'clock. The owner of the land, Mr. Rodick , was an astute businessman who encouraged tourism. Unlike other townspeople, he did not discourage the Indians from returning because he saw that it was good for trade. However, the 1890's brought the beginning of the Cottage Era and as the real estate value of the land on West Street grew, the Abenaki forever lost their place.

Today's visitors have little opportunity to appreciate the heritage of the Abenaki people, save the occasional sweetgrass basket on an antique store shelf, or birch-bark ware found in souvenir shops. However, for those who seek it, bits of history can be found. At the Jesup library there are newspapers which date back as far as 1881. Downstairs, the Historical Society has scrapbooks, photos and memorabilia dating back even further. At the Abbe Museum one can learn more about Abenaki culture and even see a birch bark wigwam. And, no matter where you go, you will be surrounded by the soaring birch trees, living reminders of the Abenaki culture and craftsmanship. 🍂

While the Abenaki rented out birch-bark canoes occasionally, they preferred to take visitors out in them. These craft, though durable and seaworthy, were expensive to build.

21

Our Cobblestone Treasury

by Tammis Coffin

Wave washed volcanic stones, rounded to perfection at a cobble beach in Acadia National Park.

COBBLE BEACHES ARE ONE of the most delightful aspects of Acadia's rocky shoreline, providing pleasure to ears, eyes and sense of touch.   A visitor to a cobble beach may hear the special music of stones rattling and rolling in the surf, or may sit upon the beach for hours, sorting through the smooth, colorful stones, looking for perfect spheres and making piles of special stones. Those who toss cobbles across the beach will find that the stones bounce incredibly high and continue bouncing for a long time with a satisfying patter.

"Cobble" is a geological term describing a rounded stone between the size of an apple and a basketball. Some of the cobbles are derived from the adjacent bedrock, but the majority are reworked from glacial deposits. Each beach presents a unique collage of rock types, a blend of local rock types and glacial erratics. The largest cobbles are cast high up by storm waves into a great wall, which spills landward after each storm.

Cobble beaches are located on the exposed shores of outer islands and peninsulas where wave action is greatest. In Acadia National Park, the cobble beaches are tucked between cliffs on the rugged southern and eastern shores of Mt. Desert Island at places like Wonderland Point and along the more remote shores of Schoodic Peninsula and Isle au Haut. The two cobble beaches that are easiest to find are Little Hunters Beach and Seawall. These may be the most accessible and most highly visited cobble beaches in the State of Maine.

Little Hunters Beach is framed by cliffs on either side and screened from the road by spruce trees. At the base of the steep log staircase lies a mound of pale-colored stones bleached by abrasion and sunlight. Where the water laps against them, the stones reveal the glowing pink of Mt. Desert Island granite and the black and grey patterns of the unusual geological formation called the "shatter zone", created when the intruding granite magma disrupted and remelted the existing rocks. Little Hunters Beach is the only beach made up of shatter zone rock, and the cobbles themselves are intriguingly patterned, layered and striped.

Many people who visit Little Hunters Beach cannot resist taking a stone along with them as a souvenir. Some park staff and local residents are alarmed over the apparent loss of volume on beaches over the years. It is said that the cobbles at Seawall used to be so high that passing motorists could not view the sea. Souvenir hunters and home landscapers have reduced parts of Seawall to an

insignificant mound of angular rocks, but still, the stones are taken away, singly and by the wheelbarrowload. Patrol Ranger Mike Blaney has noticed that beach cobbles are being removed rapidly from the park. He says, "At a place like Little Hunters Beach, we could just stand at the top of the stairs and tell people to return stones."

Maine cobbles have been steadily harvested for over three centuries. Early explorers and traders picked up cobbles to ballast their ships. Later, Maine cobbles were sought as paving stones for the streets of eastern cities. In the 1840's, John Gilley of Baker's Island regularly sailed to Boston to sell his cargo of dried fish and "popples" as they were called. Beach stones paved most city streets until the late 1800's when rectangular paving blocks replaced them. In the 1940's bargeloads of deco-

rative cobbles from Penobscot Bay were sold in a New York City department store for several dollars apiece.

The natural tumbling machine that sculpts the stones is slow and takes hundreds of years. And there won't be a new supply of stones until the next glacial age comes to pass. Let's cherish and safeguard these treasures where they lie. 🍎

Cobblestone pavement in Beacon Hill, Boston, where many of Maine's cobbles were sent in the mid-1800's.

Frederick Law Olmsted, Jr. And The Motor Roads

by Eleanor G. Ames

THERE ARE MANY WAYS to experience the wonders of Acadia National Park. One can set out on foot and hike the many trails which pass by quiet ponds and ascend mountain peaks. By horseback, mountain bike, cross-country skis or rented carriage, one can travel the network of unpaved carriage roads. Or, as is the preferred

Olmsted's diagram showing how alternative heights for curb stones would affect passenger views.

option of many visitors to the park, one can drive the Loop Road, part of a system of paved roads which give motorists an opportunity to experience many spectacular views of this remarkable landscape.

Since the arrival of the automobile on Mt. Desert Island, visitors have chosen in increasing numbers to stay in their cars. Thanks to two men — John D. Rockefeller, Jr. and Frederick Law Olmsted, Jr. — we have in the

motor roads a prime example of thoughtful design in a fragile landscape. There is much to be learned from studying the motor roads and the circumstances of their creation, in particular the thoughts and intentions of the two men who worked so hard to design them. Today, Acadia's motor roads constitute an important part of Maine's historic landscape legacy and deserve to be maintained and protected for enjoyment by future generations.

Acadia National Park has a unique history. Much of the park land was donated by private benefactors, in particular, John D. Rockefeller, Jr. The network of carriage roads was one of Rockefeller's great loves. However, by the early 1900's the automobile's time had arrived, and Mr. Rockefeller recognized that fact. He wrote to the Olmsted firm asking them to design and construct motor roads both in the park and on his private property, beginning a professional relationship between Mr. Rockefeller and Frederick Law Olmsted, Jr. concerning Acadia which was to last a decade.

Collaboration between the Olmsteds and the Rockefellers was not new. The Olmsted firm had been working with the Rockefeller family in Tarrytown, New York, since the 1800s. Beginning in 1927 they were also to work with the Rockefellers on Fort Tryon Park at the northern tip of Manhattan. Reasons other than familiarity made them a superb choice for the motor roads project. Providing a well thought-out series of landscape experiences through which the public could move without harming the landscape was a problem familiar to the firm. In the 1860s, Frederick Law Olmsted, Sr. wrote a

Olmsted designed three sections of the motor roads, while the rest, including the viaduct at Otter Creek, were planned and executed by the Bureau of Public Roads.

report on Yosemite Valley in which he considered the thorny issue of how to give large numbers of the public access to a fragile natural resource without harming it. Olmsted, Sr., and others at his firm struggled with this issue again in designing paths and carriage drives at Niagara Reservation between 1879 and 1895. Providing pleasurable access and movement through a rich natural landscape with the least negative impact was a central professional challenge throughout Olmsted's career. Olmsted had designed separate circulation systems into his many urban parks, and applied this same principle to larger scenic reservations.

Both prior to and after Olmsted Sr.'s death in 1903, his successors at the firm also addressed the issue of pleasurable access to and protection of natural resources. Indeed, Frederick Law Olmsted, Jr. wrote much of the legislation which led to the creation of the National Park Ser-

vice. The National Park Service Act of 1916 committed the Park Service to "...conserve the scenery and the natural and historic objects and the wildlife therein and to provide for the enjoyment of the same in such manner and by such means as will leave them unimpaired for the enjoyment of future generations."

Over a thousand pages of correspondence among Frederick Law Olmsted, Jr., John D. Rockefeller, Jr., George Dorr and others, found in the Olmsted Associates Records at the Library of Congress, attest to the great care which went into the design of the motor roads. This correspondence reveals an extraordinary attention to detail, a sensitivity to Acadia's vegetation and varied landscape qualities, as well as a recognition of the important aesthetic value of vistas. Olmsted and Rockefeller planned a whole landscape experience for the motor roads, in particular three areas along today's loop road known as Ocean Drive, Otter Point Cliffs, and Stanley Brook Road.

In a letter to Rockefeller in the summer of 1930, Olmsted wrote that a central problem was "to enable motorists to enjoy in high degree some of the more typi-

The Otter Cliffs section of the motor roads shortly after construction. The inside lane was elevated to permit and unobstructed view of the ocean from both sides of the road.

cal and notable types of scenery..." In 1933 Olmsted wrote *"(As) I have perhaps pointed out before, the kinds of landscapes most tellingly valuable for motorists as such are those which have a certain bigness of sweep and can be seen and enjoyed from a considerable stretch of a road by one moving rapidly along it... Amongst the most outstanding features of motor trips on Mt. Desert are some of the great views from Cadillac Mountain Road, the views out over the water from Ocean Drive, the plunging views from Otter Cliff, (and) the broad quiet views which will be obtainable from the new motor road across the Great Meadow to the surrounding mountains..."* Olmsted felt that more intimate scenery such as forest interiors and closeup views of woodland streams could not be experienced properly from moving cars. These finer, more detailed landscapes could be better enjoyed on foot.

The proposed motor road along the Tarn and the

related development of the Great Meadow as an aid to botanical research were never carried out. It was an area greatly loved by Mr. Rockefeller; designs were worked and reworked, but in the end, the project was abandoned. The motor road design work which was implemented produced spectacular results. Ocean Drive and Otter Point took full advantage of the sweeping views of Frenchman Bay. At Otter Cliffs, the superb outlook was enhanced by elevating the inner lane of road so that moving in either direction, the motorist could enjoy the spectacular view without seeing the road or another passing car. Stanley Brook Road served as the entrance from South Beach in Seal Harbor, and today remains an exquisite example of road building. Each bridge, shoulder, edge, and tree was planned along the way in minute detail. By thinning the then-existing trees and placing bridges at important points along the brook, the sequence of landscape experiences was delightful.

With the completion of the motor roads, Acadia National Park had three circulation networks—for foot, carriage, and motor traffic. The motor roads, designed to take advantage of the spectacular views and the rich varied landscape, are indeed special. Although these roads have been well maintained over the past 60 years, many of the sweeping vistas and intimate views once found along them are gone, primarily lost to the unrestrained growth of vegetation. Using currently available historic documents, including the previously discussed correspondence and over 100 relevant drawings found at Fairsted, restoration of some of these views and vistas is possible. In any event, analysis of the original intentions of Mr. Rockefeller and Mr. Olmsted can inform and educate Acadia users and admirers. Each of them in his own way left an extraordinary legacy at Acadia to future generations. It is our responsibility to protect and maintain that legacy for those who come after us. ❦

Eagles Above

by Emma Farway

The adult bald eagle, Haliaeetus leucocephalus, *with a wing span of 7-8 feet, is the largest bird in the state of Maine.*

ONE WINTER I LIVED in a house with a picture window view of Frenchman Bay. Before then, I'd often heard that bald eagles frequent the nearby islands where they nest and breed and spend their winters. With such a prime view, I began to look for them. Many times my eyes followed the form of a large soaring bird, finally resolving it to be just another gull.

My eagle watching advanced greatly when I learned that the dead tree on the end of the closest island was a favorite perch for eagles. My eyes returned to the tree again and again. Finally I saw the unmistakable outline of a real eagle.

After that, I no longer searched for eagles. They seemed to find me. I saw them every day. Whenever the thought occurred to me to look for an eagle, I'd look up or out and there one would be — soaring high in the sky above, skimming the island tree-line or cruising far out across the bay.

Several times I wished to conjure up bald eagles, to impress friends. But I did not do that, except for once. This was a private thing between me and the eagles; I might spoil it by turning it into some kind of show. One beautiful Sunday morning, though, when my visiting friend was sleeping late, I playfully called out, "Look out the window — ten bald eagles!" At that moment, to my surprise and that of my sleepy friend, an eagle flew directly past the window only a few wingspans away, the closest I'd ever seen.

My bird-watching friends assured me that they also saw eagles all the time. Yet my non-bird-watching associates did not believe it was possible to see eagles as often as I claimed.

I wondered if I possessed a special connection with the birds. Some with whom I shared these thoughts said definitely so and that the eagle must be my "totem" animal, appearing with special signs or messages that I might interpret to guide my life. Sometimes I might like to think this is true. What I wonder is, what made me look up when the eagles were there? Was my inclination to look inspired by the proximity of

27

the eagle? Or could it be because they are so close and numerous, that a person cannot help but see them?

Eventually I moved from my shoreline home and no longer had the view of the bay. I forgot about searching for eagles and stopped seeing them daily...only a few times a year or so, like most other people who live here. Recently, I told the woman occupying my former home that she could see eagles out the window and she did not believe me, although she had lived there for two years.

My specialty, when young, was in finding four-leaf clovers, and five and six-leaf clovers too. A quick search through any clump of lawn would usually yield one. It was part of the routine to sit in the grass on the sidelines of kick-ball games looking for clovers. I always had better luck than those who searched with me. Were all my four-leaf clovers making me cumulatively more lucky or did I just have better eyes?

At a recent picnic I related my former talent for finding four-leaf clovers to a neighbor. He believed what I was saying, but for some reason, as if to prove my ability, I bent over and picked up the first clover I touched - and it had four leaves!

What does a person make of all this? Perhaps I do have special powers, or maybe there are a lot of bald eagles and four-leaf clovers out there!   But, more likely, we see what we look for, and some of us are looking more than others. 🦅

The Arrival Of The Automobile

by Patti D'Angelo

BY MANY STANDARDS, Acadia is considered to be an automobile-oriented park. Many of its well-travelled roads were designed by Frederick Law Olmsted Jr. to comfortably accommodate viewers inside a moving vehicle. As each visitor season brings more vehicles over the bridge and onto Mt. Desert Island, increasingly, a question arises: How much auto traffic and exhaust can the island handle? The convenience of cars, the accessibility of roads in the park, people's inclination to view scenery from within their cars, and the small village-like design of island communities are combining to create unmanageable problems. More and more people are looking at the number of autos as one of the prime causes of our island woes.

As we enter the debate as to how or whether to control traffic flow and motor access both in the park and in our towns, we may find it useful to reflect on a question asked by an earlier generation: should cars be

Mt. Desert Street, Bar Harbor, on a Sunday in August, 1919, shortly after automobiles were allowed in the town.

29

allowed on Mt. Desert Island at all? In the early 1900's, when the popular introduction of automobiles was creating unforeseen changes across the country, the island of Mt. Desert became a social battleground between those who wanted the new automobile and those who thought it was "an infernal machine" that could only destroy the tranquil, peaceful nature of the island.

The fight was a fiery one, pitting cottagers against townspeople, shop owners against vacationers. It inspired protests, poems, and newspaper articles, and culminated with influential figures carrying the fight to the State Legislature. In 1903, a state law was passed giving voters in each town the power to prohibit cars. Autos were excluded from Ocean Drive, Bay Drive from Duck Brook to Hulls Cove, Eagle Lake Road and Green Mountain.

Main Street, Bar Harbor, before the arrival of the automobile.

Most supporters of the ban were summer residents, though many townspeople also agreed with it. After a Bar Harbor Village Improvement Association meeting in 1905, the editor of *Life,* a local weekly newspaper, reported that all of the speakers "...expressed in different words, and in different arguments, the same opinion: that the introduction here of rapid and powerful horseless carriages would prove little short of disastrous to the place..."

There were those who thought differently, insisting that the automobile was necessary for reversing the decline in the popularity of hotels. They argued that, over time, the island resort should be accessible, by auto, to more than "just... millionaires and their friends." Clearly this was a slap at the wealth and power which the anti-auto coalition employed in its fight.

During the ban, two protesters defied the law and drove their autos into Bar Harbor, where they were promptly arrested and charged a fine. One man argued in court that technically he had not driven an automobile on a town road, since he had hitched up his horse to the idle motor car and coasted into town. His defense did not stand.

The anti-auto people worried that the noisy, fuming, and often unpredictable auto would disrupt the quiet ambience of village roads and would frighten away vacationers looking for a peaceful retreat. Arthur Train, a popular writer of the time, wrote an imaginative story called "The Island of Mt. Deserted," based on his version of what would happen if the auto came to town. Set thirteen years in the future, Train satirically portrayed Bar Harbor "as a regular Coney Island, all except the camels," writing, "Everywhere could be seen clouds of dust and the air was filled with fumes of gas and the honk of horns."

Fearing that a ban applying only to certain roads would not be strong enough to deter cars permanently from Mt. Desert Island, a committee of prestigious summer people again took their case to the Maine State Legislature and lobbied for a total ban of autos on all island roads. Thus, in 1909 all cars were prohibited from island roads, forcing visitors to arrive by train, steamboat or stagecoach. Representative William Sherman, who was opposed to the bill, decried its passage, declaring "...we were snowed under by New York money."

The trend on Mt. Desert Island, however, did not mirror the trend of the rest of the country. Automobiles had taken hold in society as decisively as computers have done in our own time. The internal combustion machine was changing the way workers produced, dictated how cities grew, and was shaping transportation systems. It became apparent that no amount of influence or money could outlaw autos from the island forever.

George B. Dorr, sensing the inevitable arrival of cars, and having surveyed a prospective route for an unsuccessful railroad venture on the island, offered a compromise which eventually became acceptable to both sides. Using the surveyed railway route through Hulls Cove, around Witch Hole Pond, past Kebo Mountain and coming into town via Ledgelawn Avenue, Dorr proposed an access road for automobiles which would allow travelers to drive to Bar Harbor. When tourists arrived at their destination, they would park their cars and use horses to travel locally. Cars would still be prohibited on other roads.

The anti-auto forces, now mostly summer residents, reluctantly supported such a compromise. A bill was introduced on the opening day of the Maine Legislature in the 1911 session. Authorizing $20,000 from the town's budget towards the road's construction, the lawmakers required that the remaining funds be raised by contribution.

Meanwhile, Bar Harbor was experiencing a 10% decline in its resident population, which Representative Sherman and others argued was a result of the auto exclusion law. Southwest Harbor voted in 1911 to allow autos in town, the first island community to do so. Faced with the threat of a declining economy and the impending arrival of autos, Bar Harbor summer and town residents finally relented, repealing the exclusion law and granting total access to the town's roads. In the spring of 1913, cars were allowed in Bar Harbor. Within a few months, *The New York Times* reported that the motor car had "practically retired the horse" in the town.

The history of Mt. Desert Island's auto war may not give us direct answers to our present question of whether unmanaged car access is a burden or an asset. We can be sure that any change will bring both planned and unexpected consequences. In 1913, the decision to allow the auto led to the closing of stables and horse suppliers. New businesses began stocking auto supplies. More and more visitors arrived by their own transportation, but the waning hotel era could not be saved. John D. Rockefeller, Jr. was inspired to design the carriage roads with a permanent restriction on autos. Steamboat and train transport became unprofitable and died. The Trenton Bridge was eventually fortified to accommodate the growing influx of autos along the road we now call Route 3.

Today's decisions must be careful ones, with much at stake because of our dependence on tourism as a major part of the local economy and our struggle to maintain a precarious balance with our already strained environment.

As with those in the beginning of this century, we cannot know all the impacts of any change we implement. Keeping the status quo will also bring its own set of consequences. Who knows, perhaps "The Island of Mt. Deserted," that futuristic story about what would happen if cars were allowed on Mt. Desert Island, does hold some truth, after all. ❦

A Bar Harbor license plate.

They Oughta Be Here

by Tammis Coffin

THE FIRST SNOW OF the winter has fallen, yet the lakes are still unfrozen. Skiing along one of Acadia's carriage roads near dusk, I pause by a small pond. The snow on the water has not melted completely. A pale green layer of slush floats at the surface. I then observe that this soft surface is dotted by watery holes that resemble footprints. As I puzzle over whether they could have been made by a deer, a moose, or simply a tall person in hip waders, three dark forms break through the slush from the water below.

The sleek bodies emerge from the water, pause at the surface, arch back under, and reappear further away, all the while making new "footprints" across the pond.

The river otters found on Mt. Desert Island are elusive and seldom seen.

In the dim light, the creatures appear too small to be beavers and too supple to be ducks. They move with the grace and fluidity of seals. I feel that my presence has disturbed them, and so I ski off in the darkening night, wondering what I have seen. Only later do I realize I have seen otters.

"It is a special sighting," says Ruth Grierson, nature columnist for *The Bar Harbor Times*, though she contends that on Mt. Desert Island we are more likely to see an otter than a moose. She cautions me not to reveal the location of the sighting, as it could draw poachers, park land or not. Otters are not rare, but seldom seen. One is more likely to come across an otter if out in the woods, close to dawn or dusk.

The visitor who searches for otters at Otter Cliffs will probably be disappointed, while those who ask a native tour-guide if otter are to be found may be told curtly, "They oughta be." One certainly won't find sea otters, who inhabit the west coast of the U.S. Our river otters are a different species that only occasionally visit the ocean. Otter Cliffs are so named because of their proximity to Otter Cove and Otter Creek, which is where the otter were, or are, or *ought* to be.

River otters appeal to us because of their playfulness. They are best known for their sliding antics in mud and snow. Only three to four feet long and 10-25 pounds, with very short legs, they move easily through snow by bounding and sliding. They can swim underwater up to a quarter mile between breaths. When fishing under ice they breathe through open holes in the ice or from air bubbles beneath the surface. During the cold of the winter they often make long overland journeys to find open water for fishing. Yet, these accomplished swimmers and divers are one of the most secretive animals. Even inveterate naturalists seldom see river otters in the wild.

Because otter are elusive they are difficult to count. Nowhere in the country are their populations conclusively known. Estimates are determined by the amount of favorable habitat and by the number taken by trappers.

According to these measures, otter are doing well in all the eastern states and provinces.

A recent study by graduate student Leslie Dubuc of the University of Maine at Orono indicates that the Mt. Desert Island populations of river otter are healthy, with otters regularly using eleven of the 39 watersheds on the island. The otter do, however, alter their activities considerably to avoid encounters with humans who are their only predators. Only during winter do they venture to the shoreline to feed on a marine diet of small fish. River otter consume a wide variety of foods, including insects, snakes, frogs, freshwater mussels, snails, small fish, and even waterfowl.

River otters are usually wide ranging, covering up to 25 miles in a day. Their home ranges can include up to 50 linear miles of waterways. Yet all watersheds on Mt. Desert Island are less than three miles from their headwaters to the sea. Furbearer trapping is not allowed within park boundaries but does occur throughout Mt. Desert Island on some other public and private lands. Because otters move in and out of the park, they may be subject to trapping. Harvests have been moderate however, with an average of four kills reported per year. Most of these are taken incidental to beaver trapping.

River otters require shallow water habitat because it is a productive feeding area that also provides a protective cover of brush and tall grass for them while they forage. Otters rely on a steady water supply to maintain this type of habitat, and this ordinarily would not be possible on Mt. Desert Island, with its quick runoff and small drainages, were it not for the presence of beavers. Beaver dams provide stable water levels year round while creating shallow water habitat.

The fire of 1947 replaced the spruce and fir forest of eastern Mt. Desert Island with poplar, birch, and other beaver favorites. This led to a rapid increase in beavers who have consequently modified the watersheds, increasing the number and area of wetlands. Abandoned beaver lodges and dams provide excellent denning and resting sites for otters.

Even with the beaver-created wetlands, otter habitat on Mt. Desert Island is marginal. The short, steep watersheds are relatively low in food value. The accessibility of the ocean by the many island streams is what makes the difference in sustaining our island otter population.

It is predicted that as the poplar-birch forest slowly reverts to spruce-fir, our beaver and otter populations will decline. In the meantime, efforts of landowners to leave brushy borders along streams leading to the ocean will help the otter survive.

Because otter are so sensitive to the presence of humans, it is best for us not to go looking for them amongst our island's waterways. We may have to content ourselves with the sight of their slidemarks in snowbanks alongside the carriage roads. But if it so happens that these delightful creatures find us, we can consider ourselves fortunate. ❧

Acadia's river otters rely on the shallow water habitat created by beavers.

Movie Making On Mt. Desert Island

by Gladys O'Neil

MT. DESERT ISLAND WAS a popular location for moving picture companies from 1916 through 1921. The beautiful scenery of the island with its rugged coastline created a suitable background for many films.

The Fox Film Company was the first to come to the island in early March of 1916. Their location manager had been searching up and down the coast to find just the right place. Somes Sound, with its resemblance to a

A scene from "Queen of the Sea," *filmed in Bar Harbor in 1917.*

Norwegian fjord, provided exactly what they wanted. They intended to film one scene for a five reel production of *A Modern Thelma*, an adaptation of the play *Thelma* by Mary Corelli. The episode portrayed an old Viking dragging his daughter's betrayer aboard a ship, lashing him to the mast, sailing away from the wharf and setting the ship on fire.

The filming took place in Hall Quarry. A Bar Harbor yacht broker provided the three masted schooner. Fireworks were used to give the effect that a fire was destroying the ship while everyone scrambled to leave the vessel. The schooner was then actually set on fire and left to burn in a spectacular blaze.

This was Bar Harbor's first experience with movie folks. The actors stayed at the New Florence Hotel on Main Street opposite the junction with Mt. Desert Street. *The Bar Harbor Times* asked townspeople to be friendly and say "Howdy" if they should meet any of them around the village. Curious onlookers watched the filming and gathered about the entrance of the hotel to watch the actors leave for work in their costumes and makeup, wigs and false whiskers.

The burning of the schooner was to have been the only scene done here, but the company was so impressed with the area that they sent for the entire cast to do 34 more scenes. The leading lady, Vivian Martin, and other well known stars of the silent screen arrived during an early spring snowstorm, but it didn't dampen their enthusiasm. Snow was just what they needed for some scenes they did on Eagle Lake Road where a portable Norwegian cottage was set up to represent Thelma's home.

The Fox Film Company returned the next year to

film scenes for the *Queen of the Sea*, a million dollar epic featuring mermaids and mermen. Swimming and diving champion Annette Kellerman starred in the movie, accompanied by over a hundred actors. The scenes were filmed on Ocean Drive, and some Bar Harbor people were hired as extras, including pretty little Virginia Higgins, who appeared as the youngest mermaid in several scenes with Miss Kellerman. Many Bar Harbor residents still remember watching the scenes being filmed from the rocks along Ocean Drive.

The players remained in town for over two months and became friendly with the townspeople and the rusticators. They received many invitations to picnics, dinners and balls. People were sorry to see them leave, but they soon had the opportunity to view the completed movie at the Star Theatre. Matinee tickets were then fifty cents for adults and reserved seats in the evening cost up to one dollar. Though the movie was not highly praised by critics, it pleased Bar Harbor residents.

Photo Players Company of New York arrived next in June 1918 to film scenes along the shore at Schooner Head and Ocean Drive for Maurice Tourneur's *Woman*. Tragedy struck cameraman John Van Den Broek who was out on a ledge filming with his back to the ocean. A high wave swept him off his feet, carrying him and his camera out to sea. It happened so quickly that those on the shore were unable to help him, and he drowned as they helplessly watched. Van Den Broek was 23 years old and considered one of the best cameramen of his time.

The Vitagraph Moving Picture Company came in the summer of 1920 to film a portion of a movie being made from Hornung's exciting story *Dead Men Tell No Tales*. Again the rugged scenery of Ocean Drive was the backdrop. In this thriller, Anemone Cave was shown as the entrance to a haunted house. That fall the Post Picture Company of New York used Sand Beach as the site to film *Robinson Crusoe Hours*. Trump, a trained Irish ter-

rier, was the only member of the cast to achieve fame as he was featured in Paramount's *Tales of a Terrier*, one of the best dog pictures ever made.

In June of 1921, the Famous Players of Lasky Corporation arrived to film scenes for *Cappy Ricks*, a story by Peter B. Kyne about a typical all-American boy from Thomaston, Maine. The players included Thomas Meighan, Agnes Ayres and Thomas Malley, names familiar to all movie followers at that time. They brought with them a 325-foot steamship and several ocean-going tugs. The company waited in vain for a storm to get the effect of high winds and surf at Great Head, but fair weather deterred them, and they departed unable to complete the scenes.

Swimming and diving champion Annette Kellerman starred in "Queen of the Sea." Virginia Higgins of Bar Harbor appeared as a young mermaid.

Cappy Ricks was the last of the movies made on Mt. Desert Island by professionals, though many television commercials and documentary films have been done in recent years. Perhaps it will be just a matter of time before Mt. Desert Island will be rediscovered by the motion picture industry. ❧

Acadia's Coyotes

by Lois Winter

RELAXING ON MY FRONT PORCH on the edge of Bass Harbor Marsh, I looked up when I heard a fawn bleating its lamblike distress call. On the far side of the marsh, a few hundred yards from my house, a doe bounded through tall grass, with an eastern coyote in pursuit. I saw the spotted back of a fawn surface above the sea of grass; it appeared as though the doe was "playing interference," trying to keep the coyote away from the fawn. Apparently, the doe succeeded, for after a few minutes of chasing, the coyote ran into the woods and the doe and fawn remained in the marsh to browse.

For the past nine years, the howl of the coyote, welcomed by some, feared and misunderstood by others, has added a touch of wildness to Acadia National Park. Originally, coyotes ranged only in the western half of North America. By the early to mid-1900s, as habitat changed and wolves disappeared, coyotes began moving east. On its journey, most scientists believe that the western coyote interbred with a small subspecies of wolf in southern Ontario, creating an eastern coyote slightly larger than its western cousin. Coyotes first appeared in Maine in the 1940s but remained rare until the early 1960s. From the 1960s to the early 1980s, Maine's coyote population increased

Eastern coyotes were first documented on Mt. Desert Island in 1981.

rapidly, and by the late 1970s, coyotes were distributed throughout Maine. The narrow ocean barrier between the mainland and Mt. Desert Island may have delayed the establishment of coyotes on Mt. Desert Island; the first documented coyote sighting on Mt. Desert Island occurred in February, 1981.

How did the coyotes reach Mt. Desert Island? Contrary to popular rumor, coyotes were not introduced here by the University of Maine's Wildlife Department or by the National Park Service! After all, it only stands to reason that if coyotes managed to populate everywhere else in New England on their own, they really didn't need our help to reach Mt. Desert Island. Coyotes may have simply walked across the Trenton bridge. Or in winter, they may have walked across ice at the Narrows. In summer, a walk at low tide across the mudflats might be feasible. And although coyotes often avoid swimming, it's not unheard of. In the fall of 1990, a radio-collared coyote from the Northeast Creek area took a jaunt to the west side of the island and swam to Bartlett's Island before returning to Northeast Creek!

In anticipation of local concern about coyotes, Acadia National Park's Resource Management staff and the National Park Service's Science Division in the Regional Office contracted with the University of Maine's Wildlife Department to conduct a two-year study on the coyotes and foxes of Mt. Desert. Dr. Dan Harrison, a University of Maine Wildlife Department faculty member and the coordinator of the study, brought years of expertise to the project; in the late 1970s and throughout the 1980s, he studied coyotes and red foxes in Maine.

Field work began in Acadia in August, 1988, and

the study continued until September, 1990. Learning even a little about these elusive predators took a great deal of time and effort. Over the course of the study, three field technicians, two computer technicians, four volunteers, and I conducted howling surveys, snow-tracking surveys, scent post surveys and a summer food habits study. We live-trapped, radio-collared, and monitored the movements of 14 foxes and 12 coyotes. In addition, we entered thousands of bits of information into computers to help catalog and analyze the movements of the animals on and off Mt. Desert Island.

Prior to the study, no one knew the status of coyotes on Mount Desert Island. Are they transients or do they live and breed on the island year-round? The data we gathered confirms that coyotes are widespread on the island. From Bass Harbor Marsh to Town Hill to Seal Harbor, at least some of the animals defend year-round home ranges. And yes, coyotes breed here; results of our howling surveys suggest that a minimum of three to five families raised young on the island in 1988 and 1989.

Coyotes cover expansive home ranges. Several of our radio-collared animals range from Seal Harbor to Bar Harbor. Another ranges from the head of the island to Hulls Cove. Next time someone tells you they hear coyotes "all the time" near the Jordan Pond House and someone else tells you they hear coyotes "every night" on the Kebo Golf Course, keep in mind that both people might be hearing the same animals.

Through our research, we also hope to understand more about the dispersal patterns of juvenile coyotes on Mt. Desert Island. Dr. Harrison's studies on the mainland demonstrated that 100 percent of juvenile coyotes (between 5 and 18 months old) travelled an average of 60 miles from their birthplace before "settling down." Ease of dispersal and a low prey (deer) density on the mainland may account for the high mainland dispersal rate. High dispersal rates break up family ties and result

The howl of the coyote is welcomed by some, feared and misunderstood by others.

in a coyote social structure dominated by solitary individuals or mated pairs. Low dispersal rates, on the other hand, result in pack formation. So for Mt. Desert Island, the question remains. Do juvenile coyotes remain on the island or do they leave? Does the ocean barrier and the high prey density discourage dispersal? Although the scope of this study was not large enough to answer these questions conclusively, we gathered interesting tidbits that shed light on the questions. At least some of the radio-collared juvenile coyotes did leave Mt.

37

Desert. One left in January, 1988, and we found him one and a half weeks later in Castine. A few months later, he was shot near Augusta. Another juvenile coyote left the island and set up residence just south of Ellsworth.

In the summer of 1990, we conducted a food habits study of Mt. Desert Island's coyotes. If you've read past "letters to the Editor" in *The Bar Harbor Times*, you may remember the exaggerated fears concerning the impact of coyotes on domestic cats. Our study in 1990 confirmed results of other food habits studies conducted elsewhere in Maine and throughout North America. Although coyotes are opportunistic, their preferred food includes deer, snowshoe hare, blueberries and insects! Of all the scats analyzed in last summer's study, none included remains of domestic cats. On the other hand, coyotes regularly include deer in their diet. Even healthy deer can be fair target for coyotes, especially in deep winter snow — but that doesn't mean that the deer herd is endangered. People with little biological training often confuse the fact of predation with the effect of predation. Deer have evolved with predators for thousands

of years, and have natural ways of responding to increasing predation — by giving birth to more fawns, for example — to counteract predation and maintain viable populations.

Less commonly discussed, but a question of concern to park managers, has to do with the impact of coyotes — not on their prey, but rather, on other predators. How does the arrival of coyotes on Mt. Desert Island affect the distribution and, ultimately, the population of fox on the island? Some researchers speculate that coyotes usurp preferred territories and nudge fox into less desirable areas. Results from our snowtracking surveys, scent post surveys, and radio telemetry are helping us explore the relationship between these two closely related predators. Our preliminary results suggest that coyotes and fox tend to segregate their home ranges.

This research study — the first ever conducted on mammalian carnivores in Acadia National Park — plays a part in fulfilling the mission of the National Park Service. Only through scientific assessments of the park's wildlife can National Park rangers make wise management decisions and design effective education programs. ❦

Bar Harbor's Memorial Paths

by Gladys O'Neil

HUNDREDS OF MILES OF paths and trails crisscross Acadia National Park on beautiful Mt. Desert Island. They lead through the woods, by ponds and lakes, along streams and rocky shores, and to the mountain tops. This path system was developed and maintained for many years by the various Village Improvement Associations of Mt. Desert Island. Each organization maintained its own district within definite boundary lines.

The Bar Harbor Association began its path construction program in the summer of 1891 with the completion by workmen of a series of woodland paths designated as the Southern, Eastern, and Western groups. Sketches of these appeared consecutively during July and August in the *Bar Harbor Record*, the weekly newspaper, to acquaint readers with their location. Soon the paths became popular with early tourists. An invigorating walk in the clean Maine air came to be part of their daily routine. All of these paths could be easily negotiated by ladies in their long walking skirts.

Several new paths were built every year, and regular maintenance of the older ones was necessary. The Paths Committee was assisted by some generous members who gave Memorial Paths and often donated additional funds for their future upkeep. A few of these were obliterated by the forest fire of 1947, or eliminated because of lack of use, but most of them are still well travelled.

There is the Emery Path, the first section of the Dorr Mt. Trail, which leads up that mountain from Sieur de Monts Spring. It was given by Mrs. Alfred Anson in memory of her first husband, John Emery, a former member of the Paths Committee. The leg-stretching,

Mrs. John Innes Kane, right, with her sister, Mrs. Bridgham, at the Kane Memorial in Acadia National Park. John Innes Kane, great-grandson of John Jacob Astor, was a summer resident of Mt. Desert Island. He built the "Breakwater" cottage on the Shore Path in Bar Harbor in 1904.

high granite steps of this path remain in the memory of many a tired hiker. When the summit of the mountain is finally reached, there are good views in all directions, especially to the north and south. Directly to the west the summit of Cadillac Mountain looms, where those walking its summit's trails can look down on those looking up at the highest mountain on the island.

Kurt Dietrich's Climb, which ascends the eastern

39

Some of the many steps on the grand and historic Emery Memorial Path, Dorr Mountain.

slope of Dorr Mt. from the northern end of the Tarn Trail, was donated by his aunt, Mrs. Hunt Slater. The name is cut into one of the granite steps at the start of the trail; though almost covered by another step, it is still legible. The climber can see Huguenot Head across the small gorge to the east and look down into the Tarn.

Mrs. C. Morton Smith's memorial gift was the Beechcroft Path which leads up the western side of Huguenot Head. The trail starts east from Maine Route 3 across from the northern end of the Tarn and is marked "Beechcroft" cut in a small boulder, the same name as the Smith's summer cottage. As the path zig-zags across the ancient rock slide, fine views of Dorr Mt. open to the west.

Bronze tablets mark Memorial Paths given by other members. The Kane Path, or Tarn Trail, was presented by Mrs. John Innes Kane in memory of her husband. A small tablet designates its beginning at the northern end of the Tarn where it continues south to meet the Canon Brook Trail. A larger plaque placed a little further along the way is inscribed to John Innes Kane. He also was a member of the Paths Committee.

The Jesup Path leads from Kebo Mountain Road to Sieur de Monts Spring and then continues to join the Kane Path. A memorial tablet to Mr. and Mrs. Morris Jesup is on the right side of the path, about a five-minute walk from the spring. The Jesups were generous supporters of all the Association's projects.

Mrs. Andrew Murray Young provided the funds

for a memorial path that leads north from the Canon Brook Trail through the valley between Dorr and Cadillac Mountains, joining the Gorge Path. A bronze tablet on a huge boulder in the brook, a short distance from the beginning of the path, is inscribed "In memory of Andrew Murray Young who loved this island where God has given of His beauty with a lavish hand." The path is known today as the Murray Young Trail.

A path through The Gorge, the deep ravine between Dorr and Cadillac Mountains, was dedicated to Lillian Endicott Francklyn by a group of her friends. This path crosses Kebo Brook several times and, after an easy start, gradually becomes steeper as it passes below large precipices. A large plaque on the northern side of massive Pulpit Rock, always in deep shade, is probably passed unseen by hikers intent on keeping a secure footing on the rocky trail.

The Bates Memorial, the most impressive of all of these, was erected in 1911 by the summer residents of Bar Harbor, Northeast and Southwest Harbors to honor the former Bar Harbor Village Improvement Association president and chairman of their Paths Committee. It was placed under a pink granite overhanging ledge on the Cadillac Cliffs Trail. This location testifies to Waldron Bates' engineering skill; here the path cuts through the unusual rock formation found at the base of Gorham Mountain. The Bar Harbor Association also paid tribute to Bates by putting another tablet on a large slab of granite overhanging the Chasm Brook Trial on Sargent Mountain and renaming it the Bates Memorial Path. Bates was not the creator of the woodland paths and trails, but he devoted a great deal of his time to laying out and superintending the construction of the paths, and was thoroughly dedicated to the completion of the entire system on the island.

Even after Lafayette National Park (now Acadia) was established on the island in 1919, the Village Improvement Association continued to care for the paths. Later the new park acquired adequate funds to assume the maintenance of all those paths that were unendowed, and eventually the entire system was given into their care. Heirs of those who had given the endowment funds agreed that the money should go into the Association's general fund.

The path network is a delightful addition to this beautiful island and is enjoyed by more people every year. 🍂

Herpetofauna: Indicator Species

by Duane Pierson

"The sentinel was the first to die. But in his death the warning was struck."
                                                    — Anonymous

WHEN ONE THINKS OF the Maine woods and coastal areas surrounding Mt. Desert Island, the animals that come to mind are usually large and glamourous. These range from sea mammals like the humpback whale and harbor seals to woodland animals such as the moose and coyote. But an entirely different strata of life - wonderful species we call the herpetofauna, or amphibians and reptiles, also exist here.

Maine is a little too far north to have a richness in reptiles. The climate is too harsh for such sensitive creatures, which rely on air temperature to maintain their metabolism. Currently only four species of turtles and five of snakes can be found on Mt. Desert Island. Most of us are aware that there are no poisonous snakes dwelling within the borders of the state of Maine.

We do have a wealth of amphibians on the island. The only problem is that we do not know all we should about them. Study of amphibians on the island has been sporadic, which is rather unusual in an area where so much attention has been given to natural history. Of course, one of the problems with studying amphibians is that they are so small and secretive. There is considerable variety within species, making their identification and study difficult. And finally, to many of us, they are not that glamorous.

Amphibians include frogs, toads and salamanders and are known as indicator species. Like the legendary miner's canary, their demise tells us that trouble is afoot. Unfortunately, amphibians are disappearing on a worldwide scale. The once prolific yellow-legged frog has disappeared from California's Sierra Nevada Range. The Yosemite toad has virtually disappeared. Leopard frogs are disappearing around the country. The tiger salamander is disappearing from sites in the Colorado Rockies. The news of disappearing amphibian populations increases at an ever greater rate and is very disturbing.

Because amphibians live in both water and on land, they have evolved the unique ability to breath either through human-like lungs or through their moist skin. This means they are particularly vulnerable to environmental change. Their permeable skin entirely absorbs toxins from water and air.

There are many reasons for the decline in amphibian populations. Some disappear due to alteration of their habitat through residential and industrial development. Some die off from competition with exotic species. Many are undoubtedly susceptible to chemical toxicity whether from pesticides or acid rain and snow. And for some species there is no apparent reason for their demise.

Scientists are increasingly concerned that airborne poisons derived from acid rain and snow may be the greatest threat to amphibians' survival. But the problem is difficult to study. Throughout the world the situation is the same as on Mt. Desert Island. Herpetologists are rushing to fill the knowledge gaps about amphibian populations, their history, and their local life cycles.

Unfortunately no local group is actively working to find out exactly which amphibians are on Mount Desert Island, where they are located, and what their status is, but the Acadia Resource Inventory Project, directed by Dr. Craig Greene, a combined effort between the College of the Atlantic and Acadia National Park, is a start.

Why should we be concerned? To begin with, the removal of any local population removes a link in the ecological chain. Other species of plants and animals that depend on that species suffer by its absence, and many that feed upon it, including birds of prey, are at risk from ingesting residual toxic compounds. When we lose our most environmentally sensitive species, we receive a warning that something is wrong. If the sentinel is dead, more trouble is sure to follow. ❧

Painted turtles in the Tarn at the base of Dorr Mountain, in Acadia National Park.

For The Love Of Somes Sound

by Tammis Coffin

Somes Sound, the only fjord on the east coast of the United States, and one of many wonders of Mt. Desert Island.

IF YOU ASK ANYONE who lives near Somes Sound what they like about it, be prepared to listen for a while. Hesitantly, at first, as if they are letting you in on a secret, residents detail its wonders. They tell of the Sound's abundant shorebirds, mountain views, nesting great blue herons, deer and, the best of all, its special weather. For while neighbors a few miles seaward are grumbling in the fog, quite often people along Somes Sound are enjoying a sunny day. At night, because much of the shoreline lies within Acadia National Park, there are certain vantage points along the Sound from which no lights can be seen, taking viewers back in time.

As Somes Sound dwellers warm to the topic, you may hear of childhood journeys up "tide river" under the bridge in Somesville, glimpses of anemones the size of cannon balls, swims off sun-warmed rocks in Valley Cove, and the confidence learned by a young sailor coping with the changeable winds in the narrows off Robinson Mountain.

Almost in the same breath, residents lament the changes they have seen and warn of changes yet to come . . . fewer fish, silted shallows, fewer eagles, proposed subdivisions, more moorings, and expanding boatyards.

Somes Sound has drawn to its shores inhabitants who care deeply about the Sound and value its natural beauty and seclusion. When a salmon hatchery was proposed for Valley Cove in 1986, Somes Sound residents rallied in force to oppose the project. In short order an association was formed, substantial funds raised, lawyers engaged, scientific data gathered, and the project's permit was denied due to its threat to water quality. Next, members of the Somes Sound Association turned their attention to a variety of concerns related to the health and aesthetics of the Sound and its decline as a fishery. They hired College of the Atlantic researchers to perform water quality studies, and a few years later Acadia National Park initiated its own study.

As one would expect, results from the water quality studies indicate that Somes Sound is considered healthy, particularly in comparison to places like Narragansett Bay, but there are still many unknowns. Somes Sound's configuration as a fjord poses its own complexities and vulnerabilities owing to its extreme depth and length and correspondingly small mouth. It requires dozens of tidal cycles to flush completely, and even more during periods of heavy rain. And, though Somes Sound shares threats faced by coastal waters everywhere, because it is isolated from the open sea, it may

Changing seasons, shifting tides, clouds and light work their magic to create scenes of continual contrast.

magnify some of these problems.

Dr. Charles Roman of the National Park Service research team says that the completed chemical tests can only provide a short-term view of nutrient input within the Sound, with no insight as to trends. He recommends collecting baseline data and undertaking a monitoring program, explaining, "So little is known about the system, there's no way to tell if it is changing." Also helpful for identifying trends, says Dr. Roman, is the anecdotal evidence from people who have been around a while. What little he has heard from the fishermen he finds disturbing. Some tell of a dramatic loss of shellfish habitat since the last dredging of Southwest Harbor. Bothersome to others is the thought of what contaminants may be leaching into the Sound from two old shoreline dumps.

In their defeat of the salmon pens, Somes Sound

Whimbrel and other migratory shorebirds rest and feed in the mud flats of Somes Sound.

45

Formerly the site of a peregrine falcon nest, the sheer east face of St. Sauveur Mountain rises above Valley Cove in Somes Sound.

residents proved that they can apply considerable leverage in responding to a crisis affecting their Sound. They continue to work in a variety of ways to assure more lasting protection. Individual landowners are working with Maine Coast Heritage Trust to place permanent conservation easements on their lands. Friends of Acadia, park scientists and residents are working to expedite continued water quality studies.

For many people, Somes Sound exemplifies all that they love about Mt. Desert Island. Whether walking along Sargent Drive at sunset, picnicking atop Flying Mountain, sailing into Valley Cove, or merely glancing down the length of it while driving across the island, Somes Sound enriches all who experience it. Though Somes Sound faces the monumental problems faced by coastal areas everywhere, it does so with the determined attention and vigilance of those who know and love it well. 🌰

Excitement At The Precipice

by Emma Farway

STORM WAVES HAD WASHED out the steps, and Thunder Hole was closed. The Precipice Trail too, was closed, but I explained to my guests that there was still something very exciting to be seen there. A crowd milled about in the parking area, pointing binoculars upward and lining up to look through a ranger's spotting scope.

"It's a once in a lifetime opportunity," I exclaimed, as we joined the others in line to look through the scope. When it was my turn, with my eye pressed to the scope, I discerned a white blur — the chest of the falcon sitting on a nest. She appeared to be looking directly at us, watching warily. Despite the distance of some thousands of feet, I suspected she saw us with her natural eye better than we did her with our binoculars and scopes.

The bird on the nest was a peregrine falcon, and she was protecting three chicks, the first to be born in Acadia in 35 years. An endangered species that nearly went extinct in the 1960's, the peregrine is noted for its speed and sharp hunting skills. It has been clocked at 180 m.p.h. and can knock its prey right out of the air by the sheer force of its body.

Passersby remaining in their cars gazed upward at the cliffs, wondering what the fuss was about. Then the falcon lifted up and flew along the cliff face, and everyone could see it without magnification. All who had seen it through the scope looked upwards, shouting, "Look!"

Traditionally, peregrines and other birds of prey have not been highly regarded by farmers and hunters and were often shot as vermin who preyed on waterfowl and other more valued species. Though the peregrine falcon has the most extensive range of any bird world-

wide, the eastern United States was home to only about 350 pairs in the 1930's and '40's, even before their numbers declined.

After World War II, pesticides like DDT became widely used exterminants against agricultural pests. Not until the controversial publishing of Rachel Carson's *Silent Spring*, though, were the risks of DDT examined.

Newly hatched peregrine falcon chicks.

47

Because peregrines sit at the top of their food chain, and since DDT becomes more concentrated as it passes from host to host, the birds received heavy doses of the toxin. After over thirty years of use, DDT was banned in the U.S. But the population of peregrines and other birds had dropped dramatically; by 1964, there were no peregrines living east of the Mississippi River.

The park interpreter explained to the small crowd that from 1984 to 1986, 23 hand-reared chicks were placed in the wild at Champlain Mountain, which has the high cliffs peregrines prefer. The bird we were watching had returned here with her mate, which had been released from this very site a few years earlier.

A boy of five called excitedly to his mother, who sat in their camper, "There it is!" He was too young to know why this bird was important, but not too old to share in the excitement of spotting for himself what everyone was looking for.

One day later, as I reflected upon my view of the peregrine falcon on the nest, I remained deeply pleased that I saw the bird with my own eyes. It was a first-in-a-lifetime opportunity for me, and it may, perhaps, be the only one. I was glad that I stopped.

Peregrine falcons were the lifelong passion of my grandfather. He spent two decades of his life finding and following the "duck hawks" as he called them, locating nests, waiting for hours in blinds, photographing the ungainly young, belaying down mountain cliffs in western Massachusetts with a five-by-seven viewing camera, wooden tripod, and stacks of glass plate negatives. Once one of his cameras fell and was dashed to ruin on the rocks below. Over the years, with untiring resolve, he obtained a complete photographic collection of eggs, adults, and young. He hid nests with brush at times to protect them from his peers — ornithologists avidly interested in completing their egg collections. How well the birds tolerated his ceaseless photographic activities, I don't know, but his fascination was evident. It consumed him for years throughout the 1920's and '30's.

Through my grandfather, I have a personal connection and familiarity with peregrine falcons, born long before my first sight of the bird yesterday. Park visitors who saw the peregrines for the first time may have never heard the story of their demise and gradual recovery. Perhaps one day in the future, at the mention of the bird, some of them will remember the excitement and exclaim, "In Acadia, I saw a peregrine falcon sitting on her nest!" They will have begun the kind of relationship that my grandfather shared with me many years ago, one that can only be strengthened by the birds' return to places like Acadia. ❧

The Building Of Arts

by Gladys O'Neil

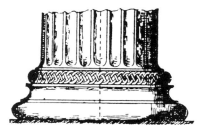

The magnificent columns of the Building of Arts dwarf theatre-goers.

THE QUIET BACK ROAD that curves through the Kebo Valley Golf course is lined by large pine trees, woods and fields. It may be difficult for the newcomer to imagine that this pastoral setting was once the site of a grand Greek Renaissance-style theatre of a scale and elegance that Bar Harbor has not seen before or since.

A group of summer residents formed the Arts Association in 1905. The group had plans to develop Bar Harbor as a center for the country's best musicians and artists, and they desired a magnificent theater in

The classic Greek style is evident in this rare photo of the Building of Arts.

which to house their productions.

The original organizers were George B. Dorr, Mrs. Henry Dimock, George Vanderbilt, Mrs. Robert Abbe, Henry Lane Eno, David Hennen Morris, and about a dozen others. The group chose a piece of land off of Cromwell Harbor Road behind the fourth green of the Kebo Valley Golf Course for their building. George Dorr, president of the association, decided on a Greek design. He had spent some time in Greece and thought that style would be perfect for their site. Guy Lowell of

Boston was chosen to be the architect.

In 1907 the building resembling a Greek temple was completed. From a distance it appeared to be of white marble, yet actually it was stucco and wood with a roof of red tile. The classic building was of simple design. The red and blue colors used throughout were similar to those used in Greece, but somewhat subdued. The auditorium seated four hundred people and included six loges. There were three seven-foot panels of plate glass on the north and south walls which gave those seated inside the impression of being out-of-doors. The building was located on an ideal natural site, with a grove of pine trees in the background and a view of Kebo Valley, the mountains and the Gorge to the south.

Opening day for the beautiful building was July 13, 1907. The first artists to perform on this stage were opera singer Emma Eames and baritone Emilio De Gorgoza. All of the summer residents attended this affair which was proclaimed a great success. The event was undoubtedly one of the most important and exciting moments in Bar Harbor's history.

The association subsequently secured great artists for summer series of concerts: Joseph Hoffman, George Harris, Ernest Schelling, Frank Kneisel, Rafaelo Dias, Carlos Salzedo, Harold Bauer, Olga Samaroff, Timothy Adamowski and Walter Damrosch.

An amphitheater was later built into the natural curve of the hill behind the building. It was here in 1916 that Vaslav Nijinsky, who was staying at the Malvern Hotel with his wife and daughter, practiced. He would be doing a new ballet that fall in New York. The Russian ballet artist was known for his ability to spring high into the air. His wife Romola, in her book entitled *Nijinsky*, writes of her visit to Bar Harbor: "There was a beautiful marble theater on top of the hill among pine woods with sliding doors. On the lawn was a Greek amphitheater where performances would be given by the world's greatest artists. Here Vaslav put Kyra (their daughter) on the lawn with her toys, slid the doors back and practiced for hours. The higher he jumped, the more she shouted for joy."

In the '30's, Hollywood and Broadway stars appeared in plays as the association tried to increase interest in the summer program. A series of foreign films was shown in 1939, but they were not well attended. Attendance had dropped gradually over the years, and the building had become badly in need of repairs.

Funds needed to restore the building could not be found. Sadly, in 1939 the building was closed.

In June of 1941 the arts building was auctioned off and bought by Charles and Earl Holt. During the summer of 1947 they sold it to Consuello Sides of Boston. She had plans to open it once again, this time as a summer theater. Before this revitalization could be accomplished, the forest fire of October 1947 raced across Kebo Valley, destroying the building. The great fire which destroyed so many of the island's treasures claimed its wonderful venture into the arts.

Now, after all these years almost every trace of the building has disappeared. It is now hard to believe that the beautiful Greek temple ever existed. ❦

In the summer of 1916 Vaslav Nijinsky practiced for hours at the theater.

51

The Harlequins Of Isle Au Haut

by Glen Mittelhauser

THE SOUTH END of Isle au Haut is a traditional wintering home for the rare, beautiful, and shy harlequin duck (*Histrionicus histrionicus*). Males of this species can be recognized by their brilliant multicolored plumage. They are a wash of blue, green, and brown with several vivid patches of white.

Harlequin ducks inhabit the northern hemisphere in both the Atlantic and Pacific Oceans. The Pacific population numbers close to one million birds while the total of Atlantic populations may not exceed four thousand. A majority of the harlequins in the Atlantic, about three thousand, breed and winter in Iceland. The others breed in Labrador and winter from Newfoundland south through the Gulf of Maine to southern New England, with concentrations at Cape St. Mary's, Newfoundland, and Isle au Haut, Maine.

The western Atlantic population of harlequins is believed to have been much larger in the early 1800's. But by 1897, in a book on the birds of Maine, Ora Knight noted a decline in the coastal Maine population and warned of extirpation of this species in the western Atlantic. In 1988 harlequins were removed from Canada's hunting list. Due to their continuing decline, they were placed on eastern Canada's Endangered Species List in 1990. Along the Maine coast, hunting of harlequins was outlawed in 1989, and they are now listed on Maine's "Watch List" of possibly endangered species.

The harlequins winter at Isle au Haut in greater numbers than anywhere else in the western Atlantic. The remoteness and inaccessibility of Isle au Haut makes it attractive to these shy ducks, but also makes field studies difficult. Little is known about their historical populations or ecology. To address this need, a study was conducted by the National Park Service and the Island Research Center of College of the Atlantic during the winters of 1988-89 and 1989-90.

Data collection techniques for this study consisted of a series of shoreline surveys on foot and by boat of Isle au Haut and nearby islands. Ducks were tallied by walking ten miles of forested, and at times trail-less, shoreline from Western Head along the southern shore of Isle au Haut, around Eastern Head and ending at Sheep Thief Gulch on the eastern side of the island. The boat surveys, conducted during calm seas, circled nearby islands east of Isle au Haut, taking great care not to frighten and flush the birds.

Harlequins did not consistently associate with other species, but were seen occasionally with large flocks of feeding common eider (*Somateria mollissima*) and black scoter (*Melanitta nigra*). Among these groups, harlequins were recognizable for their small size, and their tendency to group together close to shore where they dove for gastropods (snail-like organisms). Herring gulls were commonly seen stealing food brought to the surface by the harlequins. Usually the larger items that took time to swallow were seized by gulls.

Based on the survey results, we can now state with confidence that over 350 harlequins winter off the south shore of Isle au Haut and the small islands to the east.

The remoteness and inaccessibility of Isle au Haut affords protection for the harlequin duck, whose Atlantic population now numbers about four thousand.

Fortunately, this is nearly double previous estimates for the area. It is thought that this estimate does not represent a population increase, but rather represents more intensive and accurate census techniques.

This study provided much useful baseline data concerning the current population of harlequin ducks near Isle au Haut. Though, as is true with many preliminary studies, this one raises as many questions as it answers. For instance, what is the critical factor that makes the Isle au Haut area so attractive to the harlequins? If it is primarily the remote nature of the island, park management must be careful to regulate increasing winter use, which might be disruptive to the birds. Because of the area's importance as harlequin habitat, degradation of water quality with contaminants such as oil must be avoided, and the area should receive priority for protection should a spill ever occur.

Most important, by further understanding the harlequin's ecology, we are making steps toward the protection of this rare and beautiful bird. 🦆

A Bridge To Bar Island

by Gladys O'Neil

WOULD YOU LIKE TO be able to walk or drive to Bar Island without waiting until low tide? A bridge to the island almost became a reality in 1909.

It was at a special Town Meeting in February of 1906 that the idea was presented to the Bar Harbor (then Eden) voters by Charles Pineo. He had married Flora Rodick of the Rodick family, who were the original majority owners of Bar Island and thus represented four

View of Bar Harbor from Bar Island during the era of the great hotels. Though the hotels are now gone, the view of the mountains remains the same.

fifths of the island.

Later at a regular March Town Meeting, Mr. Pineo presented the details of the project which he estimated would cost around $23,000. Mrs. Slater, owner of the other fifth of the island was opposed to the idea of a bridge. The meeting continued into the next day. As such things usually end up, the plan was then referred to a committee to study, the idea being to find the best type of structure to be built, with a more accurate estimate of the cost.

Reporting at a meeting in May, the committee had come to the conclusion that a causeway would be the most practical structure and that it would cost $35,000 to $40,000.

Many more meetings were to be held until once again the plan was brought before the 1909 Town Meeting. There evidently was no one from the Town of Gouldsboro, in which province the island lies, to speak for or against the project. A motion to build a bridge was finally passed by voters with much rejoicing.

The selectmen asked for bids to be submitted by July 10th. All received by that time were above the amount appropriated. Mr. Pineo suggested some modification of the original plans. However, all came to a halt when July 27 brought an injunction from a group of citizens. A group of six summer residents headed by John S. Kennedy wished to prevent the building of such a structure.

On August 30th all decisions were abruptly taken out of the hands of the voters. Edward Stotesbury, president of Drexel and Co. of Philadelphia, purchased forty acres on the western side of the island. The price is said to have been well over $100,000. This brought an end to any probability of building a bridge, unless Mr. Stotesbury himself had it built.

At the time of the purchase, townspeople expected the Stotesburys would build a larger and more elaborate estate on Bar Island than any to be found in Bar Harbor. Some people had visions of dozens of other summer homes being built among the tall trees of the island, but Bar Island remained as it was.

Seven years after Mr. Stotesbury's death in 1945, the western part of the island was purchased by John D. Rockefeller, Jr. who donated it to Acadia National Park.

Yet, the building of a bridge or causeway to Bar Island continued to be a fascinating idea. In the early 1960's a serious study was made of the feasibility of such a project. However, the fact that the island is within the town of Gouldsboro discouraged anyone residing in Bar Harbor from carrying the idea any further.

Following many transfers of property on the eastern end of the island and the building of one cottage there, twenty five acres were bought by the park in 1989 for $1,000,000. Today all of the island except for one small section is owned by Acadia National Park. 🍎

At low tide one can walk across the gravel bar from Bar Harbor to Bar Island.

Bats – The Ultimate Bug Machine

by Jan Kendy

WHEN ASKED IF I would write a piece on bats, my verbal answer was affirmative and enthusiastic, but inside I was visualizing the blood sucking, snarling pets of Count Dracula! Luckily for all of us, I was very wrong, and this piece is not going to be a second rate replay of a late night trip to Transylvania.

Bats are the only major predator of night flying insects, a single bat devouring up to 3,000 mosquitoes and other flying creatures in one evening. The bad press surrounding the Hollywood "bat" myths are robbing us of the most effective, environmentally safe insect control known.

Safe? How can something that sucks blood and gets in people's hair be safe? Back to Hollywood.

Bats are not blind. They have very good eyesight, but because most of them (all those found on Mt. Desert Island) survive on tiny night flying insects, nature has equipped them with a very sensitive natural sonar that assists them in navigation and allows them to locate their prey by sound. It is called echolocation. The bat emits a very high frequency sound too high for human detection which "bounces" off surrounding objects. The nature of the sound wave coming back to the bat allows it to determine the location and identification of the object off which the sound bounced.

With a sonar so sensitive that they can locate a mosquito in the dark, and good eyesight, there goes the theory that they blindly fly into one's hair. The only reason they would even fly around one's head is to eat the insects that are also flying around one's head.

Bats are very clean, unaggressive creatures. While they are susceptible to rabies, just like all animals, according to Dr. Merlin D. Tuttle, president of the Bat Conservation Association and curator of mammals at the Milwaukee Public Museum, less than half of one percent of bats contract rabies. Unlike most other mammals, the disease does not make them aggressive. Only ten people in all the United States and Canada are believed to have gotten rabies from bats in the past four decades.

Besides being a very effective insect predator, fruit bats in the tropics disperse seeds, and nectar bats are responsible for pollinating many tropical and subtropical trees and shrubs. Dr. Tuttle indicates that the loss of bats could seriously threaten the survival of tropical rain forests.

Many of the fruits we take for granted would not exist if it weren't for bats: peaches, bananas, mangoes, figs, avocados, as well as cloves, balsa wood, manila and sisal fibers for rope, kapok for bandages and life preservers.

The authenticity of Grade B flicks exposed, I turned to Mount Desert Island. The late Stan Grierson of Bass Harbor was the president of Acadia Zoological Park and followed the bat population for many years. He rescued many from the attics of unwilling landlords. (He once told me of one colony of 400 that he had moved; 400 tiny brown bats multiplied by 3,000 insects is over a million insects devoured each night!) Alas, despite Stan's efforts and the efforts of concerned others, the bat population is definitely suffering, as a result of the development in the area. Nesting places disappear as old trees (and the hollows they contain), old barns and structures are removed or torn down.

The island is home for several bat species, but the little brown bat is the one most humans may come in contact with. They have a life expectancy of 20 to 30 years, but as a rule only produce one young each year. House cats have become a major predator of bats (as well as songbirds, toads, salamanders, shrews) and contribute to the dwindling numbers that inhabit developed areas such as ours.

Bats migrate each winter off the island, returning in April to coincide with the return of the insect population. It is uncertain where Mt. Desert bats migrate to each year, but bats in general are capable of migrating very long distances; some are known to travel between Canada and South America each year. Extremely loyal to their homesite, they could be moved many miles but would still find their way back when released.

When summer and the threat of black flies and mosquitoes approaches, the thought of one little bat devouring 3,000 insects a night certainly gives a new, more positive meaning to "bats in your belfry"! Furthermore, the knowledge that these little creatures are not blind, mean, aggressive, scary or diseased, would point to the wisdom of their proliferation as opposed to elimination. One way to encourage these wonderful natural "debuggers" is to provide nesting areas for them. "Bat boxes," the bat version of a birdhouse, can be erected facing south or southeast in an area that is safe from predators. In the state of Maine, all bats are a protected species, and extermination of them is illegal. Thus, if you are blessed with bats in your belfry, it's best to cohabit peacefully and let them do their house-cleaning on the bug population. ❦

The Great Oswald Quimby Privy Historical Site

by Oliver Quimby

MY UNCLE OSWALD WAS the proud owner of the last remaining privy in the county in which he dwelled. Despairing at seeing this once prominent fixture of rural America forever gone from the landscape, he offered it to the government along with a pretty acre of land upon which it sat.

The government graciously accepted the gift, greatly pleasing Uncle Oswald. This optimistic man had visions of the government immediately putting together a task force to administer and preserve the Oswald Quimby Privy Historical Preservation Site. Visitors from near and far would come and stare in wonder at this magnificent wooden artifact from the past. They would undoubtedly admire its quaint charm and comment upon its ecological efficiency and its compatibility with the environment.

Uncle Oswald watched for almost a year with growing sorrow and disbelief as the government did nothing but nail some "Keep Out" signs on the perimeter of the property. Mother Nature was at work staking her claim upon the land. Very rapidly wild flowers and kindred vegetation erased Uncle Oswald's decades of effort to keep them in their place.

Ultimate disaster hit on Halloween, or I really should say on one of the days following Halloween. Some pranksters tipped over the outhouse. Uncle Oswald noted this and smiled. Some things never change as kids had done this every year that Oswald could remember, including one year long ago when Aunt Molly had taken a seat and was busy reading the Sears and Roebuck catalog by candlelight. The ultimate tragedy occurred a few days after the latest tipping when

a fleet of state trucks with accompanying bulldozer showed up at the site. The dozer easily smashed the ancient structure and then proceeded to busily move dirt about the site. The trucks and their green clad attendants made a morning of picking up the splinters, enjoying a nice coffee break, and engaging in what appeared to be a lot of intensive conferring on matters one could only assume to be of great importance. Where Uncle Oswald arrived at the scene he asked in his politest language (learned during a four year World War II stint in the Marine Corps) why they had done what they just did.

It was officially explained to Uncle Oswald, a bit too pompously for his taste, that someone had upset the privy and that the good state workers had rectified the situation by obliterating it. Oswald informed them that the upsetting happened every year and that all they would have to have done was to set it up once again and it could once again be handsomely silhouetted against the sky.

After much staring at the ground and a little glancing about, the head man stated that such a course of action was impossible as there was no money in the state budget for placing fallen structures upright and that there was only money for demolition and removal. Uncle Oswald did not realize it but he had run into a very common phenomenon. He had left something of value to the state without leaving an endowment to perpetually care for it.

One of the basic rules of the universe is that while government is very good at gathering things in, it isn't very good at taking care of them once it has them. Uncle Oswald is not the only one to find this out

A once prominent fixture of rural America.

through hard experience. A multitude of good people have given prized possessions to government at every level only to see them forgotten, not cared for, ill-maintained, and/or neglected. Let's not jump to the conclusion that government is devious or intentionally deceptive. Government reminds one of a child who wants things given to it but has no means of taking care of them. And like a child, it thinks, "Maybe next year we'll finally have a lot of money so we can fix things up and take care of everything we own."

Over the decades many wonderful citizens here on Mt. Desert Island and on our neighboring shores have given many fine things to the government — land, buildings, carriage roads, trails, artifacts, easements, etc., and the government has accepted them giving back promises and thank yous. And like Uncle Oswald's privy, they simply let these gifts sit and deteriorate as dreams are dreamed of big budgets and found money.

The lesson in all this is that you cannot give something to the government without also giving government the means to maintain it. Somehow that sort of defeats the purpose of the idea of gift giving. But, that's the way it is. You could talk to Uncle Oswald about this, but he is at rest in a piece of ground, paid up front for perpetual maintenance. ❧

We are left only to guess at the site of the Oswald Quimby privy.

Acadia's Woodpeckers

by Ruth Gortner Grierson

TAP, TAP, WHO'S THERE? Here, in Acadia National Park on Mt. Desert Island, it could be any one of eight woodpeckers. Commonly seen residents are the downy and hairy woodpeckers, both with a red patch on the back of the head—like a small and large size of the same woodpecker; the flicker with its flashy white rump patch; the large flamboyant pileated woodpecker with his flaming red crest; and the yellow bellied sapsucker. Less frequently seen is the black backed woodpecker and rarely seen are the American three-toed and the red headed woodpecker.

These unique birds do not tap idly in our woods. They are declaring their territories or advertising for a mate. Or they could also be making a nest cavity or just telling the neighborhood that they are around—saying "I'm here, I'm a woodpecker!" Woodpeckers will tap straight sometimes or will use alternate blows delivered slightly from each side, like a woodman with his axe, as they chisel out a piece of wood. These birds spend hours tapping away, usually on a tree but sometimes on a metal sign, and then there really is a racket. Their chisel tipped bill is a good tool for excavating a nest and for probing for food; and with their incredible tongues they can reach far into an ant's nest.

A woodpecker's tongue is very special and it is so long in some cases that it curves inside around the back and top of the skull. The free end is armed with barbs or spines so wood boring larvae may be impaled and then drawn out of the hidden tunnels in tree trunks.

Common yellow shafted flicker, one of our island's eight woodpeckers.

Slender bones support this long tongue, and they slide in a sheath that extends around the back of the head and over the crown. The tongue is attached to the front of the bird's mouth, and a sticky coating of a glue-like substance on the end of the tongue insures that an insect is caught if the tongue finds it. In getting their food, woodpeckers rarely disfigure a tree, for the birds can locate hidden prey with great accuracy. They do not do exploratory surgery. The trees usually swell and heal over later.

Drumming is one form of communication but woodpeckers also give visual messages. Flickers have a white rump patch they display as they fly off. This is a signal for others to follow, or it can act as a danger signal, like the deer's flashing white tail. If a woodpecker wants to threaten an intruder it will erect the crown or crest feathers, aim its bill at the intruder and say with these motions, "Leave!" These interesting birds use both vocal and body language to get their ideas across.

The downy is the smallest of the woodpeckers seen here and is a familiar visitor to bird feeders. The bird is feathered in black and white with a small red patch on the back of the male's head. Its tweezer-like bill and small size distinguish it from the similar looking but larger hairy woodpecker. Downies spend hours banging away with their pointed bills, making holes and pulling insects out. If a hawk should threaten one, the downy will escape by dodging around the tree or by flattening itself on the branch. Wait a moment or two, though, and it will start moving again.

Hairy woodpeckers look like a size larger version of the downy. You are more apt to hear a hairy drumming in late winter and spring, for pairs of birds drum in duets early in the year. Pairing occurs in the winter and breeding in March and June. New pairs seem to have more to say to each other, and they do a great deal of drumming. One female being studied drummed hundreds of times a day, 54 times in five minutes, as she advertised for a mate. The nest hole of the hairy is special, for the bird makes a square hole for a doorway which is often on the underside of a limb. Hairies are expert carpenters of bird-dom as well as protectors of fruit trees and woodlots.

The flicker is our only woodpecker with a brown back, but it is the white rump patch, red patch on the back of the head and black crescent on the breast that identify it. Since ants are its chief food, you see them often alongside the road as they probe into ant colonies to retrieve these insects on their incredibly long, sticky tongues. Five thousand ants have been found in one bird's stomach! The introduced European starlings have taken over flicker nesting holes in many areas and have decreased our native flicker's numbers considerably.

Although the yellow bellied sapsucker is the butt of many jokes, the name is accurate. It does have a yellow belly and it does drill holes for sap. The bird actually digs its own wells in trees, making a regular series of pit-like holes most often on the shady side of a tree. As the sap collects in the opening, the bird wipes it out with its tongue. A sapsucker's tongue has half brush-like tips, rather than sharply pointed ones like other woodpeckers, and this bird eats more vegetable food than the others. Insects attracted to the sap flowing will be eaten by many birds, and even squirrels come to drink at the holes.

Woodpeckers as a rule have four toes, but the black-backed woodpecker and the American three-toed woodpecker have three toes on each foot. The black-backed woodpecker has been recorded nesting here, but

The different forests of Mt. Desert Island provide habitat for a variety of woodpeckers.

61

Spring apple blossoms.

Woodpeckers rid fruit trees and woodlots of wood boring pests.

The biggest member of the local woodpecker group is, of course, the pileated woodpecker. Startlingly patterned in white on a black background and sporting a vivid red crest on top of its jaunty long-necked head, it does not go unnoticed. The holes made by this bird tell you it is in the neighborhood before you actually see this extraordinary woodchopper. The rectangular holes made by this crow-sized woodpecker are dug in ant infested trees or rotten logs containing beetles and larvae. Its principle food is carpenter ants. Pileated woodpeckers used to be birds of the deep woods, but they have now adapted to more populated areas and chop away at logs on lawns close to houses and along busy streets.

Occasionally, a red-headed woodpecker makes a surprise appearance on the island, most often in the fall and late spring, but this is not a bird to expect very often. As its name implies, the adult bird has a completely red head, not just a red patch. Immatures have a brown head, but both adult and immature will have a wide white wing patch to help in identification.

All woodpeckers are hard working, substantial citizens rendering a most valuable service to our trees, and they are well equipped with highly specialized tools for their lifestyle. Wherever they live, they leave behind striking evidence of their presence by their holes in dead trees, and they let us know they are about by all that tap, tap, tapping. 🦗

the American three-toed is a rare visitor. It is interesting to watch the often-tame black-backed woodpeckers flipping off pieces of bark on live and dead spruces as they look for grubs lurking beneath the bark.

Leaving old trees standing is important for helping woodpeckers of all kinds, as well as other birds, to find food and/or nesting sites. It is not always wise to "tidy up" the woods nearby.

Does Anyone Remember Red Rock Spring?

by Gladys O'Neil

HARDEN FARM at the foot of Kebo Mt. was often called Harden Park. Its grassy fields, surrounded by mountains, formed an idyllic, park-like setting similar to Robin Hood Park (Morrell Park) close by. It was a beautiful spot where there was also a bubbling spring of pure, sparkling water beneath a stand of tall white birches. The spring had always been an asset when the Hardens had farmed there, but it wasn't until financial problems arose in 1902 that John Prescott, the heir to the property, decided to turn it into a commercial enterprise.

The spring was dug to a depth of nine feet and lined with pale blue tiles. There was a layer of cement five feet square outside of the tiling and a wall of red granite. The ground beyond this had been excavated to the depth of the spring and filled with screened gravel, over this was a flagging of granite. The curb of the spring was of red rock from the red granite quarry on the property. An immense trough, also of red granite, was placed in the bottling house, and it was from these pieces of granite that the spring was given its name.

At the bottling house the water was either bottled plain as it came from the spring or charged by carbonator into a sparkling drink. It was sold by the gallon or half gallon, in bulk, carboys and bottles.

Fame of the water's purity and fine flavor spread to all parts of the island and the business grew quickly. The majority of Bar Harbor's hotels and cottages were supplied with Red Rock Spring Water. The water could also be made into all kinds of delicious soft drinks by adding pure syrup flavorings, and people living hundreds of miles away were able to enjoy summer beverages such as ginger ale, sarsaparilla and others.

In 1906, the Red Rock Spring Water Company was organized with Charles Burrill as treasurer and Thomas Searls, president. The company's name was changed again to Mount Kebo Spring Water Company in 1907.

"Pure, palatable and portable," were the words used to describe the spring water in the company's advertising during 1908, and the beverage became so popular that a sales representative was appointed in New York City.

An attractive trade mark, a large key crossed with a bow, was adopted in 1910, and it was used in all of their advertising thereafter.

The business continued until 1929 when all 50 acres were purchased by George Dorr who gave the land to Acadia National Park.

Many Bar Harbor people still call the area Red Rock Spring. ❦

The label design from a Mount Kebo Spring Water Co. bottle.

An old bottle found on the ocean floor near Bald Porcupine Island is all that remains from a picnic long ago.

63

Offshore Islands

by Tammis Coffin

The cool, moist climate and barren rocky terrain of Maine's offshore islands create a suitable habitat for plants and animals normally found much further north.

Double-crested cormorant.

UNINHABITED, BARREN AND FOG-SWEPT – Maine's offshore islands evoke a sense of mystery. In appearance, their landscape resembles the Labrador tundra. Approaching them, there is the thrill of the unknown and a chill at the prospect of being stranded on the inhospitable-looking rocks, surrounded only by miles of cold sea. Close to their shores, signs of life appear — stems of purple iris nod in the sea breeze, puffins duck into crannies, and guillemots stream forth from crevices within the cliffs.

Acadia is a park made up almost entirely of islands. Of the thousands of diverse islands that make up the

There are about 3,000 islands off the coast of Maine. Most represent an intact coastal wilderness.

coast of Maine, the park owns just over a dozen. The largest of these, Mt. Desert Island, is the most popular, most accessible and most well known. The others, lying further offshore, are largely uninhabited and occupy only a small fraction of the park's acreage.

Offshore islands tend to be somewhat fragile, often harboring sensitive ecological zones and plant and animal species that may be endangered, threatened or otherwise worthy of special management concern. The cool, moist climate and barren rocky terrain create a suitable habitat for sub-arctic types of plants normally found much further north, such as oyster leaf, roseroot stonecrop, beachhead iris, and the diminutive blinks.

The isolation and absence of predators on small offshore islands provide breeding places for such rare seabirds as the Leach's storm petrel, razorbill, Atlantic puffin, and roseate and arctic tern.

The increasing popularity of sea kayaking and small boating make small islands particularly vulnerable to human impact. Yet these smaller islands are some of the least studied resources in the park.

In order to enhance our knowledge of these places, a special team of researchers assisted Acadia National Park in performing inventories of the small islands in the summer of 1992 and 1993. Schoolteachers volunteered

The rare beachhead iris flowers along the Maine coast from early June to mid-July.

Harbor seals 'haul out' on ledges at low tide to rest, soak up some sun, and nurse their young.

through the organization "Earthwatch," as part of a National Park Service initiative. The volunteers helped determine the species of plants and animals found on the offshore islands, including the types of sub-arctic plants and breeding birds.

The Earthwatch teams worked with Acadia National Park's resource management staff to establish transects for long term monitoring and collected baseline data to be used in assessing long term change, climatic effects, and the effects of "acid fog."

A question of immediate interest to Acadia National Park resource managers concerns the designation of cultural and natural management zones on the small islands. Baker Island, for example, was settled in the 18th and 19th century and represents an important chapter in the history of coastal Maine. Sheep historically grazed on Baker and on many other islands now managed by the National Park Service. Sheep may be considered as a future alternative for maintaining cultural landscapes, but before sheep are re-introduced, it must be determined which plant and animal species will be affected by grazing.

All those involved in this worthy effort hope that the collected information will stimulate further research on these fragile offshore islands. ❦

The Stone Tower On Great Head

by Gladys O'Neil

IN 1910, J.P. MORGAN, one of the most prominent bankers in the world, bought Great Head and Sand Beach as a gift for his daughter, Louisa Satterlee.

The Satterlees built three bungalows above Sand Beach. They also erected a barn and superintendent's house near Schooner Head Road.

A stone tea house tower was built in 1915 on the top of Great Head, one of the highest headlands on the Atlantic Coast. From this site the view is spectacular, especially of Frenchman's Bay and the eastern shore of Mount Desert Island.

Building a structure at this site was no easy task, but was accomplished with the help of Melba the donkey. During her labor, she traveled a total of five hundred miles carrying thirty six tons of sand and cement up the rough trail to build the tower. Later, Mrs. Satterlee rewarded Melba with all the good things that donkeys like for the rest of her life.

The stone tower was fifteen feet high and eighteen feet in diameter. The flat roof featured a railing for an observatory. This roof was reached by a ladder within the tower. Inside the structure there was a spacious tea room with a wooden floor and a stove.

In the great fire of 1947, the three adjacent bungalows were destroyed and the tower itself was damaged by the firey plumes that raced across Great Head and finally plunged into the ocean. Two years later, Great Head and Sand Beach were given to Acadia National Park by the Satterlee's daughter, Eleanor.

The remains of the tea tower were torn down later for safety reasons, but the foundation of the building can be seen atop Great Head by hikers who take the steep trail from the eastern end of Sand Beach or the easier path which leads from the parking lot on the old Schooner Head Road. ❦

Satterlee Tea House that once stood at Great Head, overlooking Sand Beach.

67

Tiptoeing Over The Mountains

by Tammis Coffin

Beehive Mountain and the pond at 'The Bowl,' viewed from Champlain Mountain.

WHEN WE CLIMB THE mountains in Acadia, we take for granted that we can tramp across bare rocks in vast open windy places. We like the freedom to walk anywhere on the summits with the sun in our hair and the breeze in our faces. The stone cairns scattered about give us a sense of ease and the license to wander about and enjoy views from every prominence, to north, south, east and west.

But our wandering is changing the mountains. A man I know has a favorite mountain that he has enjoyed climbing for most of his life. After leaving Mt. Desert Island for seven years, he returned to find his mountain transformed. The borders of vegetation that formerly lined the path up Beech Mountain had receded. Familiar shrubs such as the sheep laurel with its pink blossoms, the low-bush blueberry, and huckleberry seemed less abundant. Areas of bare rock and loose gravel trail appeared to be widening, while the areas covered by plants appeared to be shrinking.

Our mountains are showing wear. "People say, 'Wow, things are changing here!', but you have no way of really knowing unless you measure the change," says Acadia National Park's botanist Linda Gregory. Linda has worked with Dr. Mary Foley of the park service regional office to document the types and amounts of plants on Acadia's mountain summits so future changes can be monitored.

The mountain tops were barren of trees in 1604  when explorer Samuel de Champlain gave this island its name, which translates from French to "Island of Barren Mountains." Most of these bald domes will never sprout a forest. The combined effects of glaciation, fire burns, and runoff have left scanty amounts of soil. Yet many small plants and shrubs cling to the crevices and pockets on the rocky mountain slopes.

The cool, barren summits of Mt. Desert Island, bathed in frequent summer fogs, afford habitat for plants normally found at much higher elevations and northern latitudes. Among these are rare subalpine plants such as the alpine clubmoss and a delicate plant with white flowers called mountain sandwort.

Mountain sandwort (Arenaria groenlandica) *a rare sub-alpine plant found on Acadia's barren summits.*

Mountain soils are hard-earned and scarce and the plants upon it have a tenuous hold. When human footsteps loosen soil on slopes, rainfall can then wash it away. The result is that the small islands of vegetation begin to fray around the edges. As the area covered by soil and plants recedes, it bares the rocks, and paves the way for washouts, gullies and accelerated soil loss.

There is beauty in the miniature plant arrangements found on lichen crusted mountain ledges, particularly in fall, when the blueberry leaves are a coppery red, the wine-leafed cinquefoil turns to burgundy, and the sheep laurel is streaked orange and yellow.

Stepping stones along a trail near the Tarn, facing Huegenot Head.

When you climb a mountain try to avoid stepping on the plants or soil. Instead, when possible, try to step from stone to stone along the trail. This may require a bit of practice and no small measure of agility, but over time it becomes a habit. Every well placed footstep matters and will help to keep intact the mountain landscapes we enjoy, with as much beauty to be viewed at our feet as there is to be seen off in the distance. ❦

The Moose Who Summer Here

by Tammis Coffin

MOST EVERYONE WILL TELL you there are no moose on Mt. Desert Island. To find them you have to go north, to moose country — the great north woods, where that great animal roams. Moose need lots of wilderness, a full square mile each.

It comes as a surprise to learn that for the Abenaki Indians, this island, which they called "Pemetic" (meaning sloping land) was a choice spot for moose hunting. The young Abenaki men returned here on special moose hunting expeditions each fall after the rest of the tribe went upriver to harvest their plantings of corn. Here at Pemetic the moose were hunted by being driven into the water with lighted torches and shot with bow and arrow while swimming. Although all of the moose was used, smoked moose tongues were highly esteemed.

In the years that have followed, Mt. Desert Island has changed and the moose have moved on. But oddly enough, every few summers, a moose or two return to spend their summers here. When moose appear, they are most often seen along roadsides near Seawall, where they leave great cloven footprints. Stepping majestically into the road in the dim light of dawn, they have startled boatyard workers on their way to the early morning shift at Hinckley's.

One of our more memorable moose visitors in recent years was a cow a few summers back. She was reported to the police as a wild horse running loose at Seal Harbor beach, she was observed nibbling at a Somesville garden, and later seen swimming in Eagle Lake by Acadia National Park's newly arrived Superintendent on his first walk down to that lake shore.

Though moose generally prefer the solitude of the wild, they have a reputation for bumbling into unlikely places. A Portland (Maine) newspaper headline from 1927 reads: "Couple Treed by Moose Five Miles From Portland." Other entries from the same year state: "Bull Moose Ambles on State Highway Ignoring Traffic" and: "Bull Moose Lassoed by Taxi Driver."

Moose have poor vision and rely almost entirely on their sense of smell. The sheer size of moose, with legs longer than most of us are tall, leaves a lasting impression. Despite their clumsy appearance and sizeable rack of antlers, moose are expert swimmers and divers and they move through dense woods with stealth and ease.

Even though Mt. Desert Island's wild areas are relatively small, the moose who come here manage to stay hidden from most of us, although several have had fatal encounters with speeding autos or poacher's guns.

That moose still come here, stay all summer long and even bear their young (as happened recently) almost strains the imagination. Their

71

Bass Harbor Marsh is one refuge for moose that come to Mt. Desert Island.

presence recalls a time we thought we left long ago, when unbroken forests covered all the coast of Maine and birch bark canoes plied our shores. We have kept enough of this island's wildness intact to satisfy this great beast, at least for its occasional visits. Let us welcome the moose kindly in hopes that they will always return. 🍃

The Story of Duck Brook Bridge

by Gladys O'Neil

LEAVING BAR HARBOR TRAVELING north on Route 3, the traveler is granted a brief glimpse of a magnificent stone bridge. This high, triple arch span is known as the Duck Brook Bridge. All of the bridges in Acadia have their own story; the Duck Brook Bridge is perhaps the most fascinating of all.

The bridge you see is one of many stone bridges that link the Park Loop Road. Their construction spanned nearly a decade, a time marked by war and the devastating 1947 fire. The loop road itself was finished in 1941, but when World War II was declared all work ceased on National Park roads and bridges. It wasn't

Under construction – the massive Duck Brook Bridge along Acadia's Park Loop Road, not to be confused with the Duck Brook Bridge that is part of the carriage road system.

73

Quinn, of Bar Harbor were the winning bidders for this massive construction project. The work began in August of 1950. It took two years to finish this span which rises 100 feet above the brook.

The Duck Brook bridge was designed by the Bureau of Public Roads for the National Park Service. The construction itself was an engineering feat. The bridge has an overall length of 402 feet from one side of the ravine to the other and is made up of three arches measuring 89 feet, 95 feet and 89 feet, with approaching spans of 65 feet on either side. To support these arches during construction, the Timber Structure Company of New York designed 42 wooden trusses which were shipped knocked down from Portland, Oregon. Assembled on the site, the trusses were lifted into place by a boom and crane. These were erected without a single "centering stick". In order to avoid using any centering mark under the top members of the rugged frames, which made up the backbone of the construction, the contractors placed pairs of timber trusses from wall to wall.

A miniature railroad, known as the "M & M" railroad was constructed to carry 16-cubic-foot concrete buggies used to transport the concrete when pouring the arches. As the concrete was poured, the wooden trusses supported a weight of 800 tons. Although this structure is made of steel and concrete, the exterior facing is pinkish gray granite, hauled from Halls Quarry 12 miles away. Each section was cut piece by piece on the site by expert stone cutters and put into place like the pieces of a giant jigsaw puzzle.

The statistics of the project were impressive: 92,000 hours of labor were spent on the job with as many as 75 men working at one time; 4300 cubic yards of concrete, 400,000 pounds of reinforcing steel and 1,100 cubic yards of stone were used. All of this for $366,000!

At a simple ceremony on October 8, 1952, the last

until 1950 that construction resumed. By then fire had swept the area leaving it devoid of most trees.

Duck Brook flows from Eagle Lake and empties into Frenchman Bay just below the Sonogee Estates on Eden Street. Most of the land crossed by the new Park Loop Road was donated to Acadia National Park by John D. Rockefeller, Jr. He expressed the wish to have a bridge built in keeping with the beauty and grandeur of the island.

The M & M Construction Company, consisting of W. Robinson Martin of Manchester, Vt. and Harold Mac-

600-pound piece of granite was put into place, completing the largest bridge of its kind east of the Mississippi and one of the prettiest in the country. The road was opened in July of 1953 and is known as one of the loveliest drives in Acadia.

The next time you leave Bar Harbor going north on Route 3, slow down after you pass the C & N ferry terminal and take a look to your left to see the magnificent bridge spanning the Duck Brook ravine. 🐿

Two views of the bridge shortly after completion in 1953.

Snowshoe Hares Of Mt. Desert Island

by Patti D'Angelo

A winter scene in Acadia National Park.

IN 1931, NINE HUNDRED snowshoe hares were taken from an area near Seawall and transported live to Pennsylvania trappers. This note, recorded in the *Journal of Mammology*, may make one wonder if hares are still plentiful, and if they are, where they can be spotted most easily. Learning more about *Lepus americanus* will reveal some clues to their whereabouts on Mt. Desert Island.

Snowshoe hares' most obvious distinctions are its changing fur color and its large hind feet. Both of these features enable it to live in northern climates beyond the range limits of its relative, the eastern cottontail. The snowshoe hare is brown in summer, with a white belly, and in winter the tips of its fur whiten, except for its upper ears. With its elongated back feet, this hare can travel easily over fallen snow.

The hare is larger than the eastern cottontail and has longer ears. There are more subtle differences between these animals, as well. When a female hare has a litter, her young are furred, their eyes open, and they can move within minutes. A cottontail's litter is unable to survive without the constant presence of its parent until the young are a few days old.

The snowshoe hare goes through highly fluctuating population cycles, which explains why the numbers recorded in the '30's may not reflect today's population. Their predators here are primarily coyote, fox and owl.

Swamps, forests and brushy areas are the snowshoe hare's favorite habitat, and an individual hare will use a winter range of only a few acres, depending on the availability of food. The hare uses this range so extensively that snow can become packed down on the network of paths it uses. This familiarity with its territory is an extra benefit when escaping predators, who do not know the area as well. Snowshoe hares generally take cover during the day, bedding down in "forms," hollows where snow cover is shallow, wind is scarce, and the sun penetrates the shrub cover. At night, they forage on buds, bark and twigs of saplings and shrubs, as well as leaves and grass in summer.

A hare's habits reveal certain signs to the alert observer. Twigs and branches about one or two feet above the ground that are cut at a 45 degree angle were almost certainly eaten by snowshoe hares. In addition, scat identification can be a ready hint to winter tracking. Hare scat is small and oval-shaped and consists of partially digested plant matter. In winter, hares will sometimes eat their own scat to gain more nutrition from the tough fibers of bark and buds.

The tracks of the snowshoe hare are easily distinguished, with their long outside hind prints and round inner front paw prints. When a hare gallops, it places its hind feet ahead of its forefeet. As its speed increases, the hare lands with its forepaws in a single line, not as a pair, like a squirrel does.

A winter-time walk or ski on Mt. Desert Island reveals tracks of the snowshoe hare in the snow almost everywhere, though one seldom sees the snow-white hare itself. During a winter with little snow, the hare is quite visible and somewhat amusing, hopping across a brown landscape. Though we may laugh, we can congratulate the hare's earnest preparations. After all, it is winter and snow is surely soon to come. 🐾

Lepus americanus, the snowshoe hare common to Mt. Desert Island.

Bar Harbor's Village Green

by Gladys O'Neil

THE VILLAGE GREEN in Bar Harbor wasn't always a park. In 1868 it was the site of the Bay View Hotel, built by the Hamor family with their cousin, Edward Young. After being enlarged several times the hotel became part of the Grand Central Hotel complex.

In 1899 the town purchased the property from Johnston Livingston for $45,000, a price many voters thought was too high, particularly as no one was sure what should be done with the land. The now dilapidated hotel building was torn down with some of the reusable lumber saved for constructing the Young Men's Christian Association building the next year. The debris was soon cleaned up leaving a large empty lot.

It wasn't long before a group of people raised $89 to build a bandstand on the vacant lot, though another $40, would be needed before the bandstand could be finished. The first concert was played there on July 21, 1899.

Except for the bandstand, the property lay idle for three years, when the town's building committee chose the location as the site for a new grammar school. No sooner had the excavation for the school's foundation begun, than they decided that they had made a mistake. At a special town meeting it was voted to cancel the building contracts and to construct the new school on Ledgelawn Avenue. Five hundred dollars were raised to clean up the lot once again.

It now appeared that a better use of the land would be to make it into a park. The *Bar Harbor Record* suggest-

Mr. and Mrs. William Roberts donated the large granite seat facing Main Street in 1907 in memory of their son, John Whittington Roberts.

ed that it be named Hamor Park, dedicated to Eben Hamor, one of the town's earliest citizens who had done so much for the village. It would also serve to honor the Hamor family who had built one of the town's first hotels. However, the park continued to be called the Town Lot or the old Grand Central Lot by most people, and eventually became known as the Village Green.

Years passed and nothing was done to improve the appearance of the town's newest property. Finally, the Village Improvement Association took action to clean up the property and make it more attractive by leasing it from the town. In 1905, Morris K. Jesup brought this about with the help of a committee.

Everyone in town seemed enthused about the improvements planned for The Green. Shrubs were given as a gift from school children, trees were planted as memorials to family members, a seat around the large tree at the entrance to The Green was given as a gift, and benches were purchased by the Association.

Mrs. John Harrison (Chairman of the Village Green Committee) gave the watering trough at the corner of Main and Mt. Desert Street in 1906. Mr. and Mrs. William Roberts donated the large granite seat facing Main Street. It was placed there in 1907 in memory of their son John Whittington Roberts, who died in 1904. In the same year a cement garden seat was the gift of Clavin Norris. Some Association members paid to have trees transplanted from the old school lot on Cottage Street. The Association donated a granite bench with V.I.A. (Village Improvement Association) cut into one side which faced Mt. Desert Street.

In 1908, a Winter Festival was conducted by the Association to raise funds for the yearly upkeep of The Green. Summer festivals were regularly held after this first event and were very successful.

Many monuments have been given to the Village Green over the decades. Some have lost their meaning while others have been lost altogether. The granite seat facing Mt. Desert Street marked M.E.F. (for Mary Ellis Farnum) was given by Mrs. John Peltz's mother in memory of her sister, the former Mary Ellis Bell, who had died in 1894. A bubbling drinking fountain placed in back of the watering trough was donated by a friend of The Green in 1917. During 1927 a flagpole placed on the northeast section of the park was moved nearer the fountain. A plaque given by Mrs. Herbert Washington in memory of her husband and sister was laid on the ground in back of a tree near the watering trough in 1928. It is not known if this denoted a special gift.

In 1909, Philip Livingston gave a bronze fountain in memory of his wife. Sculptured by an Italian artist it was from an estate near Florence, Italy. For many years water had not flowed through the fountain. Through the efforts of a group calling themselves Friends of the Fountain, money was raised to restore the fountain and install new plumbing. After two years of effort, in the summer of 1992 it was a working fountain again. A diagonal path had been laid across the lot in 1910, making easier access

Philip Livingston gave this bronze Italian fountain to the Village Green in memory of his wife in 1909.

79

to Firefly Lane and Mt. Desert Street.

In 1920, Sunday afternoon concerts were given by the Boston Symphony Orchestra. The program from four to six o'clock was well attended, but it was during the warm summer evenings that crowds filled the Village Green. A dance pavilion had been built entirely by volunteers on a piece of town property across from The Green on Firefly Lane. There was dancing to the music provided by the Boston Orchestra playing in the bandstand on Wednesday nights, while the Bar Harbor Band performed on Tuesday and Thursday nights.

The lease of the Village Improvement Association was renewed and The Green remained under its care until 1923. In 1921, the Association hired the famous landscape architect Beatrix Farrand to improve the landscape of the property. She had a barberry hedge removed that had been planted to border the diagonal path. The bandstand was moved back from the path and lowered. It was rebuilt on the site in 1972.

In 1945, the town erected a large bulletin board on a grey granite background with the names of Bar Harbor men who served in World War II. The design of the memorial proved to be impractical as more wars followed. This was replaced in 1977, by a bronze plaque honoring both men and women who had served their country. This was a gift from the Village Improvement Association who also moved their granite bench from the lawn and placed it in front of the memorial, improving its appearance.

The Village Green is always a busy place during the summer. In recent years it has been the site of art exhibits and craft shows. Recently, it has suffered from overuse and is in need of restoration and long term care. In the fall of 1992, a Village Green Committee was formed to join with the Village Improvement Association to bring this restoration about. Donations are being sought from those who care about this park and want it to look its best again. History goes on and on as do the summer nights, repeating itself but never quite the same. 🐛

On warm summer evenings crowds filled the Village Green to dance to the music of the Boston Symphony Orchestra and the Bar Harbor Band.

The Village Green, Bar Harbor, Me.

Bar Harbor, Maine. The Village Green from Main Street

The De Gregoire Family Of Hulls Cove

by Gladys O'Neil

THE LONG CONFLICT BETWEEN England and France for the possession of Acadia prevented settlement upon the disputed territory by settlers of either nationality for many years.

In 1688, King Louis the Fourteenth of France granted all of Mt. Desert Island to Antoine de la Mothe Cadillac in recognition of military service Cadillac had rendered in America. Cadillac died around 1719, after having gone on to settle Detroit, but having never taken possession of his land here on Mt. Desert Island.

Cadillac's grant was revived nearly a hundred years later when his granddaughter, Madame Marie Thérèse de Gregoire and her husband Barthelmy, came to America seeking claim to his property. The fall of Quebec in 1759 had put an end to French domination of the area, and the first permanent settlers had already begun to arrive on Mt. Desert Island.

The de Gregoires arrived in Boston in 1786 with their three children Pierre, Nicholas and Marie, bringing with them letters of introduction from Lafayette and Thomas Jefferson. Madame de Gregoire presented her claim before the General Court of Massachusetts. Though the claim was old and doubtless obsolete, the magic of Lafayette's name and the positive sentiment towards France at the close of Revolutionary War had a favorable effect. On July 6, 1787, she was granted the eastern half of Mt. Desert Island and some land on the mainland, with the exception of select holdings taken by earlier settlers. The whole family received naturalization by a special act of the legislature.

The de Gregoires found that they were unable to sell their land while in Boston and became so deeply in debt that they had no recourse but to come to Hulls Cove in 1788. There they built a small house and tried to farm. Being rather elderly, unaccustomed to rural life, and unable to speak English, the de Gregoires were nonetheless well-liked by island inhabitants. They sold some land with deeds issued for 100 acre settler's tracts at $5 in "milled gold pieces" for a de Gregoire title. However, it was not enough to meet their debts. Finally in 1806, they turned over their remaining property to one Royal Gurley in exchange for an agreement to support them for the rest of the lives. It is believed that their children returned to France around 1800. Barthelmy died in November of 1810 and Madame in 1811, and they were buried in the Hulls Cove cemetery.

In August of 1889, The *Bar Harbor Record* printed an editorial telling the de Gregoire's story and suggesting that the people of Eden (Bar Harbor) donate funds to build a monument at the site of their grave in Hulls Cove. It was pointed out that nearly every property owner in the town could trace their title to the two French settlers who were at one time owners of almost the entire town and that it would seem but fair that those who profited from their land do a little to rescue their last resting place from oblivion.

A small granite stone with the name de Gregoire and the date 1811 cut into it was later placed on the

Antoine de la Mothe Cadillac, pioneer founder of Detroit, Michigan and former owner of all of Mt. Desert Island.

Most of what is now Acadia National Park was once considered part of the de Gregoire estate.

grave by Miss Cornelia Prime, summer resident of Hulls Cove, and in 1958, a plaque was dedicated by a group of Bar Harbor residents to mark the location of the de Gregoire's house that reads:

> *Site of the American home of Thérèse de Gregoire to whom half of the island of Mount Desert was granted in 1787 by the Commonwealth of Massachusetts as heiress to the French title through her grandfather Antoine de Mothe Cadillac.*

At one time the grass-covered outlines of the cellar of the de Gregoire's house could be plainly seen, but the area is now overgrown. The boulder with the plaque still sits there on the little hill overlooking the Colony Motel in Hulls Cove.

A simple monument located in Hulls Cove is all that remains to remind us of the de Gregoires.

Lest We Forget

by John Kauffmann

NATURE IS THE HEART and soul of Acadia National Park. A matchless combination of scenic beauty and other natural values form its essential reason for being protected.

It was the reason why artists and lovers of the outdoors were attracted to Mount Desert Island in the first place and, in the words of historian Sargent Collier, were "determined to preserve for posterity the original splendor of one of the most excitingly beautiful sections of the country."

Acadia was to be and is a *nature reserve,* but in a recent television program a past park superintendent termed its scenery merely "pleasant," and intimated that cultural features, namely the park's outstanding system of trails and carriage roads, are the only resources that really make the park world-class. Perhaps he forgot park history and may not have accurately appraised the qualities that brought Acadia into the National Park System.

Those impressive trail and road constructions are themselves of first rank, magnificent indeed in concept and quality, and they add tremendously to the interest, significance, and the enjoyment of the park. They are servants to the beauty here, however, providing appropriate access for enjoyment of an astounding array of natural features. That was and is their facilitating purpose. Were it not for Acadia's outstanding natural attractions, it is doubtful that such excellent roads and trails would have been built.

They have been much talked of lately because of their plight. People who loved this island deeply gave of their time, energy, and money to build a system of more than 200 miles of beautifully constructed trails. Only

Everything here brings joy to the soul of the observer.

83

about half of them remain open. John D. Rockefeller, Jr., personally provided the vision, oversight, and funds for 57 miles of carriage roads of superb quality and architectural excellence. There is probably nothing finer anywhere on public land. He *gave* them to the nation, and the nation has let them deteriorate. That is the reason for the great concern.

Nevertheless, concerned recognition and respect for those and other historical resources here must not allow us to forget, not ever, that Acadia is first and foremost a combination of natural features unmatched anywhere in such a concentrated collection. Although he bridled at a poet's pat dictum that Mount Desert is "the most beautiful island in the world," Freeman Tilden, one of the pre-eminent park interpreters of our time, went on to declare that "the description utterly fails to do justice to this rock-built natural fortress which thrusts forward into the Atlantic and challenges its power." "Everything is here to rejoice the soul of the human visitor," he declared.

Showy Lady Slippers.

In its classification of units of the National Park System, the Park Service lists Acadia not as an historical park, a cultural one, or in the recreational category, but as a *natural* area. In Tilden's book *The National Parks,* he begins discussing Acadia in the context of the story of glaciation, the ice age being the latest major sculptor of the island. The story is far richer than that, he indicates, for "this is a place where you can stand with one foot in the brine and one on the blossomy land."

Russell Butcher sums it up in his *Field Guide to Aca-dia National Park:* "Just on this single island," he lists not only the glaciated mountains but also a score of lakes, Somes Sound, rich and varied forests, more than a hundred species of wildflowers and flowering shrubs, brooks, bogs where rare plants grow, countless harbors and coves and islands dotting the bays and ocean. Northern and temperate life zones overlap in downeast Maine, and the bird life is accordingly rich. "The island's 108 square miles embrace some of the most varied and charming scenery of any area of comparable size in America." Butcher concludes.

After vainly searching maps to find anything like Mount Desert Island anywhere, one can but agree with Freeman Tilden that Acadia is unique.

So what do we do with what Tilden termed a "protected, preserved haven for all the people?" We must treat this small treasure very carefully; tread lightly; approach softly, quietly. Acadia's rocks are tough but its plants are not. Its solitude, its peace is even more easily disturbed. Yet that is its best balm and delight: the quiet places, the savored vistas, the small exquisite assemblages of plants and water and stone. Incredible as it may seem in such a circumscribed environment, Acadia even offers wilderness values in its small recesses. These are the special blessings that Acadia can bestow if safeguarded.

Management of Acadia should therefore emphasize the gentle, appreciative ways of visiting. The essence of Acadia can never truly be attained by automotive means, which too often disturb and degrade it. We should be thankful and caring for the walking paths and the carriage roads— bike ways and ski ways as well as horse ways now. They lead us handsomely into the unique combination of natural beauties that makes Acadia a National Park. Above all other values, those natural elements deserve and need our most cherishing respect and protection. They must always remain sovereign here. 🐾

The Bear Island Light Is Lit

by Jack Perkins

THE BEAR ISLAND LIGHT shines once more!

This historic lighthouse at the mouth of Northeast Harbor, its light extinguished by official decree eight years ago, has been given new life thanks to the efforts of Friends of Acadia.

Formal relighting of the 150-year-old coastal fixture occurred on a foggy evening in August of 1989, the weekend that also marked the 200th anniversary of American lighthouse service established under order of President George Washington, and the bicentennial, as well, of the town of Mount Desert, off which the Bear Island Light is located.

Officials of the National Park Service, which has custody of the island, and the Coast Guard, joined members of Friends of Acadia at relighting ceremonies. There would have been a marine parade with hundreds of boats circling the lighthouse, live radio broadcasts from a Coast Guard cutter reviewing the parade, a dedication by Senator George Mitchell, whose efforts on behalf of those who would restore old lighthouses are

The Bear Island Light, a welcoming beacon at the entrance to Northeast Harbor.

well documented, and a spectacular fireworks display to mark the moment of relighting, BUT—

Fog did us in! The grand ceremonies had to be scrubbed! But, on signal radioed from the mainland, two Park Service employees on the island flipped the switch and the light began flashing each five seconds through the murky night.

Friends of Acadia could celebrate. All those who had led fund-raising efforts to support Bear Island Light could rejoice. A bit of Maine coast history was reborn.

Actually, our efforts on behalf of the old lighthouse structures had begun a year earlier raising monies to restore and stabilize the roof of the keeper's house adjoining the light to prevent further destruction.

Bear Island, under lease to private owner, can be enjoyed from the water.

Then, the question was asked: Why not relight the light? Why not, indeed.

A task force from Friends of Acadia met with Coast Guard officials to determine feasibility and procedures. Since the Coast Guard, in deciding to decommission the light years before, had declared the Bear Island Light no longer needed for navigational purposes, we would have to either present persuasive arguments that it *was* needed, or undertake permission to restore the light as mere-

ly a private operation. That's the course chosen.

Coast Guard personnel, familiar with lighthouse technologies, were generous with time and expertise. The light that had been removed from the tower might be replaced but new equipment, now available, would be much better.

Recommended: a stand alone, solarpowered system. Single solar panel affixed to the deck of the lighthouse. Twelve volt deep-cycle solar battery. Clear white, flashing light, .55 amp, set to flash for a half second each five seconds. All control equipment automatic, photosensitive, darkness triggering the flashing of the light, a carousel of spare bulbs, the device able to sense when a bulb has burned out and rotate a fresh bulb into firing position. No people required, save for annual maintenance checks which Coast Guard personnel volunteered to handle.

Friends of Acadia arranged purchase of this equipment. Acadia National Park Superintendent Jack Hauptman, actively interested throughout the project and largely responsible for its successful conclusion, assigned staff to process paperwork and eventually to manage the physical installation of equipment.

So that, finally, fog or no fog, when that August night came, it was Superintendent Hauptman who led jubilant Friends in the celebratory countdown—four, three, two, one! ! !

And the Bear Island Light, so long dark, flashed forth once more!

When next you see it, think of Friends of Acadia, think of what people, working together, can accomplish, think of the specialness of this part of the world where the Bear Island Light once more lights the way for our ships and our souls. ❦

A Question Of Quality

by Oliver Quimby

"No one goes there anymore. It's too crowded."

–Yogi Berra

WHAT IS QUALITY? Since antiquity, philosophers have attempted to answer this question. And, I must say that none of them has done too well. Even Plato took a crack at it and came up without a very good answer.

I cannot tell you what quality is; but I do know what it is when I see it. Don't we all? I do think we can agree on a couple of points related to quality. The area of Mt. Desert Island and its environs is a unique distinctive area which has traditionally offered to those who love it, quality of experience and lifestyle. Unfortunately, when something of quality exists everyone wants at least a part of it, and many people will relentlessly exploit it. Consequently, when something of quality and beauty is shared by everyone, it seldom remains something of quality and beauty. And finally, what we have here in the area of Mt. Desert Island is something precious which more and more people want, placing it in danger of becoming something else.

Mr. Berra's famous aphorism at the start of this essay very succinctly states what becomes of quality places. They experience a shift in demographics. What was once exclusive, a place for a privileged few, becomes a mecca for the masses.

We must be careful here. We dwell in an egalitarian society, one supposedly devoted to free enterprise. Words such as privilege, exclusive, excellence, and elite have become proscribed. They are available to everyone, and every person can do what one pleases with one's property (with minor restraints).

One can write an interesting but sad history about the hundreds of once quality places throughout America that were discovered and became "used to be's." An excellent example of this is the entire New Jersey shore.

Can we save a precious resource from being destroyed by the very people who love it?

No matter what town one visits there, you hear stories of how it used to be way back when, before it was discovered and exploited, becoming but one more strip of sand, backed by countless souvenir, T-shirt, and ice cream shops. Paradoxically, each of those places still brings happiness to thousands of people and profit to numerous entrepreneurs. But that ephemeral thing we call quality is gone with most of the natural beauty. What remains is only a taste of what once was, an attraction built on the myth and an essence of the past.

I cannot say this is all bad. But I can say it could have been different. Suppose there had existed planners in mid-nineteenth-century America and civic leaders with uncanny foresight. And suppose these people had said, "We are going to protect this beautiful coastline. Visitation of all types will be controlled. Domiciles and hotels will be constructed well back from the shore and off the barrier islands. And, shops, arcades, restaurants and such places will be encouraged but consigned to certain areas under architectural and landscape codes indigenous to the tradition of the region." If all that had been, the New Jersey shore would have remained one of the true natural wonders of the continent available in all its beauty for all generations to come.

Fortunately for us, most of our Maine coast remains as it has always been. This does not mean that it has not been discovered. Recently, the front page of the *Sunday New York Times* travel section featured Acadia National Park and advised visitors to avoid Mt. Desert Island as it is too crowded and to instead visit Isle Au Haut and the Schoodic Peninsula. Thanks a lot, but I guess that's what being a travel editor is all about — sending people to quaint forgotten places so they will no longer be quaint and forgotten.

Acadia National Park has long been discovered.

Only one thing has saved the park and the area from being thoroughly inundated with people and all the tacky accouterments of mass tourist trade. That one thing is lack of accessibility. It remains an effort to get here, regardless of the mode. The easier it becomes to reach the area, the more it will change.

And yet, despite the inaccessibility, the number of visitors continues to increase. This happens for a host of reasons including more publicity, more incentive for the casual visitor (shops, fast food, amusement rides, etc.) to make the trip, and a lack of alternatives in the Northeast. With every increase in visitors, the demographics

A red admiral butterfly alights on rough-fruited cinquefoil flowers.

change. One type of visitor drives out another. As local merchandising adjusts to meet the new visitor type, it promotes more of the same and chases away the old. A transition takes place that is barely perceptible whereby an upscale clientele is replaced by one that has lower expectations and needs. This is not to be critical of one over the other, but to state that a change is taking place in the area of Acadia National Park that is similar to that having affected numerous other once beautiful scenic areas.

Nor can we say that any category of people is more deserving than another due to economic status, recreational tastes, or whatever. Where our interest becomes intense is when the forces engendered by visitation, both numbers and types, threaten the quality of the area. Such threats manifest themselves through ecological impact, resource destruction, aesthetic devaluation and even a decline in property value. What it is that was once here will be no more, and masses of people will come only to grasp at the shreds of something once beautiful and precious.

Can we preserve an item of quality, can we save a precious resource from being destroyed by the very people who love it?

The answer is yes, but it can only be done through control. Museums and art galleries have always done it. What we have to do here in the area of Acadia National Park is to make a collective determination that we want to protect this area and that we are not going to let other people or forces take it from us. It is our only course. 🍏

Interrupted ferns grace the woodlands, meadows and swamps of Mt. Desert Island.

Blazing Trail

by Oliver Quimby

WHEN IT COMES TO the marking of trails, experts abound. Among our hiking friends we can identify four distinct trail marking species, the blazers, the cairn builders, the cairn removers, and the bushwhackers. Though they barely tolerate one another's systems, they, each in their own way, see that as we wend our way along the merry trails, we get lost through no fault of theirs.

Gone forever are the days of the hatchet wielding blazers, lustily hacking their way through the forest primeval. Perhaps aesthetics were to be found in manly swings as gash led to gash. The modern blazer goes out with paintbrush and can of gaudy pigment, dabbing, daubing and splotching his or her way through the wild wood and over the lofty crag. All those who follow can find their way carefully marked by fluorescent speckles until that spot where any type of marking would be most welcome but all that is encountered is a challenging lapse.

Then we have that unique species who for some reason is compelled to gather up loose stones and arrange them in piles. One rock pile points hikers to the next, and so on, across the hills. Somewhere in the soul of these builders is imprinted the sanctity of rock piles. The cairn builder considers his or her self an artist and, like most artists, deigns the work of others. And so they build their piles, each one a monument to something, we know not what. There is great satisfaction in building cairns, this we do know.

Is there really beauty in a pile of rocks, no matter how artfully constructed? Many of us think so even though when we need to, we cannot recollect what utilitarian symbols the various forms convey. However, there are others among us who feel that anyone who displaces a rock upon our hallowed ledges despoils nature's beauty. With as much ardor as the builders, they tear these piles apart and scatter them back to how they think nature intended things to be.

Finally, we have that wanton purist of the wilderness, the bushwhacker. No one is going to show this person where to go and what to do. Self-propelled, these rugged individualists plunge across the terrain, finding direction only by sun, stars, instinct, and moss on the trees. Once they tried a compass, but the darned thing made no sense. No person will follow this person's trail, not even a search party seeking the recently disappeared.

Our search for the perfect trail marking system continues on. Perhaps one day we will have a hologram-laser system where each of us wears a miniature laser seeking out holograms concealed upon trees and rocks. But that will stand no chance against the blazers who prefer red paint, the blazers who prefer white, the blazers who prefer the tin animal cut-outs nailed up on trees, or the cairn builders. To keep it interesting, we will contend with the cairn destroyers and the bushwhackers. We can expect the debate to go on, without setting direction, never failing to amuse. 🐾

A Future For Farmland

by David MacDonald

HOW DOES FARMLAND FIT into the diverse natural and cultural makeup of Mount Desert Island? When most people think of this region, the images that come to mind are of Acadia's mountains, lakes, woods, and shoreline. The farms, however, are essential to the Island's "sense of place" and the health and well-being of the area communities.

Agricultural lands provide locally-grown produce, scenic open space, and a link to Maine's agrarian past. As large, relatively undeveloped tracts of land, they also serve as significant wildlife corridors and act to buffer many natural resources preserved within Acadia National Park's boundaries. Most importantly, these farms represent our only hope for continued local productivity in the future. Their "prime soils" are a limited resource—the agricultural equivalent of an endangered species.

In order to provide a clear picture of the agricultural land base on Mount Desert Island and to encourage a better understanding of how to preserve these important lands, Maine Coast Heritage Trust conducted an inventory of farmland on Mount Desert Island in 1990.

Using the definition, along with U.S.D.A. soil survey maps, aerial photographs, tax maps, and the advice of landowners and town employees, Maine Coast Heritage Trust identified approximately 65 plots of farmland on Mount Desert Island, totalling 3,341 acres. This means that 4.8 percent of Mount Desert Island is farmland, compared to a figure of 6.6 percent statewide.

Site visits and questionnaires distributed to landowners brought more detailed information about which farms are currently active — 1,215 acres are actively being farmed and 2,126 acres are considered inactive, but available for future productivity

Twenty farms on Mount Desert Island are active. They raise hay, fruits and vegetables (including strawberries, blackberries, blueberries and herbs), and livestock such as goats, pigs, cows, horses, sheep, rabbits, chickens, and ducks. These farms employ the equivalent of 27 full-time workers. Most of the agricultural products raised are sold or swapped for use on the island by restaurants, grocers, florists, wreath-makers, and local consumers.

The threats to our farmlands, a non-renewable resource, are very real. Owners face constant financial pressures that, in the words of one farmer, "make it a lot simpler and more attractive to sell out than struggle to make ends meet." High property taxes, low profits, lack of farm labor, high cost of equipment, building and maintaining structures, and the cost of land itself, all contribute to the plight of local farmers.

The threat to farmland is increased by the fact that it possesses a number of qualities that make it especially attractive for development. Specifically, farmland tends to be easier and less expensive to build on than land which has to be cleared of trees, levelled for building sites, and filled for septic systems. Also, farmland usually has scenic quality, further increasing its likelihood for conversion.

Findings from the inventory show a small but vital agricultural land base on Mount Desert Island that is subject to intensive growth pressures. Landowners share great concern about the future of farming on the island, but most express hope that with the cooperation of towns and residents, agriculture can remain viable here.

What exactly is a farm? Everyone thinks they know, but definitions can vary widely. As defined by the U.S.D.A. Soil Conservation Service, "farmland" is a tract of land that has the soil quality, growing season and water supply necessary to sustain the raising of livestock or crops. Farmland encompasses currently or historically productive land that can provide for partial to full sustenance of individuals farming the land.

Despite their many concerns about the future of farming on the island, most farmland owners surveyed believe that with adequate community support and understanding, agriculture on Mount Desert Island can survive. "I think the small, local farms will come back, but it's going to take a whole new thought process," wrote one landowner. Others suggested that local farmers will be helped by agricultural zoning, property assessments and tax rates that are more in line with a farmer's income, and allowing farmers to sell produce directly in downtown areas.

Throughout the inventory, Maine Coast Heritage Trust has been encouraged by the amount of input provided by farmland owners and also by a high level of interest in farmland protection shown by towns and by Acadia National Park. Bar Harbor, the town with the largest agricultural land base and the most active farms on the island, intends to develop policies that encourage farmland preservation as part of the town's comprehensive planning process. One of the town's goals is to promote the use of conservation easements. Conservation easements are voluntary legal agreements that place permanent restrictions on the use of properties, while allowing the land to remain in private ownership.

Three important farms in Bar Harbor have already been permanently preserved, thanks to the landowner's decisions to voluntarily limit future development in the form of conservation easements. Maine Coast Heritage Trust continues to assist a number of other farmland owners who want to protect their properties' special features that provide important public benefits.

Beyond voluntary land protection initiatives on the part of individual farmland owners, much depends on the desire and ability of local communities to support agriculture on Mount Desert Island. You can help by becoming more involved in your town's comprehensive planning process, by letting your town officials know how you feel regarding this matter, purchasing locally grown produce, and contacting Maine Coast Heritage Trust for more information on the results of the Inventory of Farmland on Mount Desert Island.

Maine Coast Heritage Trust is a private, non-profit land conservation organization offering advisory services to landowners, land trusts, and other organizations and agencies such as Acadia National Park.

Monument Cove

by Tammis Coffin

MONUMENT COVE IS ONE of the great wonders of Acadia National Park, though few who drive by it ever know of its existence. A cliff-lined enclosure opens up to a broad expanse of ocean and an unbroken horizon. Off to one side of the cove, there stands a solitary granite pillar, the "monument" for which the cove is named. Granite boulders nestle around the monuments base, boulders remarkable for their size, pink color and roundness.

Though the monument is impressive, some claim that its spire is getting shorter each year. Whether a casualty of natural forces, or if daredevil climbers are to be blamed, something is apparently causing the monument's slow demise.

Besides the prominent monument, what makes the cove exciting is its spectacular beach made of boulders, one of the few to be found along the entire coast of New England. To have granite blocks the size of pumpkins be so beautifully rounded and so smooth, is a rarity and a marvel.

The coarse-grained pink bedrock of Ocean Drive happens to contain several sets of cracks or "joints" that are vertical and near vertical, along with more closely spaced sub-horizontal "sheeting fractures," or cracks. This arrangement of fractures and joints permits large blocks to be naturally "quarried" by the waves into large rectangular blocks. Winter waves along this shoreline are strong enough to tear these gigantic blocks loose, break them into square-like blocks and round off their corners into great spheres and ovals.

It is difficult to imagine how someone could carry any of the forty pound boulders up the cliffs and out of the cove. Though it is now illegal to remove stones from the park, one finds pink boulders of matching size and shape decorating lawns and driveways throughout Bar Harbor. As the years pass, the stones sink into the grass and become covered with moss.

Some have wondered aloud what Monument Cove would look like with all of its purloined stones returned, if indeed that is where they originated. For now, I would say the stones are safe, nesting on local lawns, though perhaps someday a plot will be carried out to return them to their point of origin.

There was a family who summered on a nearby island for generations who collected many beautiful beach boulders to take home with them to the mid-west. It wasn't until they moved one year that they found what a pile of stones they had amassed. Very thoughtfully, they decided to return them to where they belonged. The family made a special pilgrimage to Maine and carefully marched the boulders back to the beach, one at a time.

What price tag might be affixed to the boulders ornamenting lawns and decorating the shoreline of Maine? Certainly they are rare, and for sure, it takes a long time for them to be formed. But the boulders in Acadia are protected, and Monument Cove is where you can look at them. ❦

Old engravings refer to the cove's granite spire as "the obelisk."

Moments Of Wonder

by Emma Farway

NEARLY EVERY VISITOR TO Acadia National Park has a special walk or place in Acadia, or a time of year or season when the park appeals to them in an indelible special way, moments that become awash with colors, or rich in scents, textures, or the unexpected.

A couple I met said they come each night at sunset to the shores of Witch Hole Pond. "The wood ducks return to the pond to spend the night," they whispered in hushed tones. I had hoped to rustle through the bushes along the shore to pick huckleberries until the

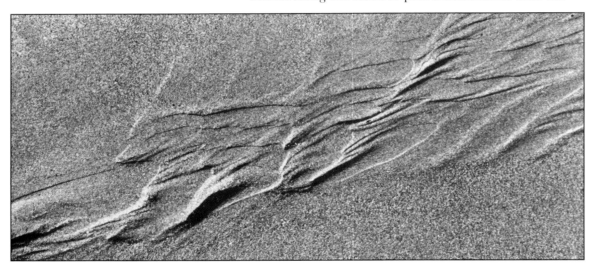

Wave-etched patterns in the sand at Sand Beach, Acadia.

last light gave out, but I moved on in respect for their reverent greeting of the wood ducks.

My friend Mark likes to speak of the time he went skating after dark on Eagle Lake on a moonless night. The sky and the ice were black; he skated into the darkness with the white rounded curves of the mountains reflected in perfect double on the ice before him.

One visitor, struck with wonder by the beauty of the rock cairns and the stunted junipers and cedars on the open rocky ledges of Cadillac Mountain said, "It almost feels like a Japanese garden that's meant to be a reflection of nature, but this is actually like the nature that the gardens are trying to reflect."

One still morning in late summer, while hiking up the east slope of Dorr Mountain, I looked out across Frenchman's Bay to see miniature clouds banking up against and nearly concealing each of the small Porcupine Islands. These delicate ghost-like apparitions soon vanished, and I never saw them again.

And there are the carriage roads, designed to grace and frame the natural beauty of Acadia. As Ann Rockefeller Roberts writes in her book, *Mr. Rockefeller's Roads,* "On the carriage roads, the walker proceeds through a sequence of 'events', each carefully chosen to reveal the park's landscape to its greatest advantage. It is possible to see sun rise and set from these roads; to see back to the mainland and on a clear day discern distant Mount Katahdin; to see the sun shimmering on the ocean from the shoulder of Sargent Mountain; to behold the clouds reflected on Jordan Pond."

From an aerial perspective Acadia National Park appears like a stage set from Disney. The mountains are exaggerated in profile and appear almost like great loaves of bread rising from the ocean. The expanse of rocky ledges and mountains and their proximity to the moist cool sea, create a wondrous range of experiences in Acadia, new with every change in weather, and in every change of light. 🍎

Credits

page 80: postcards courtesy of the Bar Harbor
Historical Society
page 81: photo courtesy of the Bar Harbor Historical Society
page 82: large photo courtesy of *The Bar Harbor Times*
small photo courtesy of the Bar Harbor Historical
Society
pp. 83, 84: photos courtesy of *The Bar Harbor Times*
pp. 85, 86: photos from Friends of Acadia files
pp. 87-93: photos courtesy of *The Bar Harbor Times*
page 94: photo courtesy of Acadia National Park
pp. 95, 98: old engraving, Friends of Acadia files
pp. 96, 99: photos courtesy of *The Bar Harbor Times*

We regret that since our efforts to trace the identity of some photographers and artists whose work has been reproduced remain fruitless, the above list is not complete.

Acknowledgements

THE RUSTICATOR'S JOURNAL is a compilation of articles that have appeared in past issues of the Friends of Acadia JOURNAL. The book represents a labor of love by many people who care deeply about Mount Desert Island and Acadia National Park. We thank all of the writers, artists and friends who graciously donated the articles, photographs and art work that appear in this book.

We give a very special thank you to Gladys O'Neil of the Bar Harbor Historical Society, for her steady stream of articles and her assistance in locating old postcards and photographs in the historical society archives.

We thank Earl Brechlin, Editor of *The Bar Harbor Times* for generously giving us many of his own photographs and allowing us access to the newspaper's photo files.

We thank Raymond Strout of Ahlblad's frame shop who loaned us many of the old engravings that illustrate the book, and we thank Frank Matter of Acadia Publishing for allowing us to reprint articles which previously appeared in his publications.

Those who provided critical assistance in checking facts and locating illustrations include Eleanor Ames of the Maine Olmsted Alliance, Nina Gormley of the Wendell Gilley Museum, Elizabeth Igleheart of the Maine Historic Preservation Commission, Reverend Edwin Garrett of the Bar Harbor Historical Society, and Ruth Grierson.

We are grateful to the following individuals for their help in proofing the text: Binnie MacDonald and Caroline Reeb and our indexer Nicholas Humez. Gail Dunn provided crucial administrative support. Patti D'Angelo provided invaluable assistance in helping to select and edit articles.

Special recognition goes to Karen Zimmermann of Z Studio. We owe her our sincere appreciation for her creative design work. And we thank her for her patience and cooperation throughout our countless revisions.

Proceeds from the sale of this book will go towards Friends of Acadia's efforts to help preserve the beauty, character, and experience of Mount Desert Island. We thank all those who support Friends of Acadia and who help make our work possible.

Tammis Coffin & Duane Pierson
Friends of Acadia
June, 1993

Index *by Nick Humez*

104